USDA

United States
Department of
Agriculture

Forest Service

Forest
Products
Laboratory

General
Technical
Report
FPL–GTR–146

Log Sort Yard Economics, Planning, and Feasibility

John Rusty Dramm
Robert Govett
Ted Bilek
Gerry L. Jackson

Abstract

This publication discusses basic marketing and economic concepts, planning approach, and feasibility methodology for assessing log sort yard operations. Special attention is given to sorting small-diameter and underutilized logs from forest restoration, fuels reduction, and thinning operations. A planned programming approach of objectively determining the feasibility of establishing a log sort yard operation is recommended. This critical thinking will help develop the strategic, marketing, business, and operational plans to guide the development and operation of the log sort yard. Preliminary financial feasibility should begin early in the planning process to help focus efforts on potentially viable opportunities and save time, effort, and money from chasing poor investment scenarios. After options are narrowed, detailed resource assessment, markets, and financial analyses are done. Several critical factors are considered and evaluated for each log sort yard scenario. Although commercial log sort yards have a proven track record throughout North America, small community-based and government-operated log yards have had limited success. Serious consideration must be given to employing an experienced log sort yard contractor to operate and manage day-to-day operations. Several operational, policy, and judicial issues need to be resolved for successful operation of government and community log sort yards in the United States.

Keywords: log sort yard, small-diameter, economics, feasibility, marginal logs, community log sort yard, government log sort yard, planned programming

February 2004

Dramm, John Rusty; Govett, Robert; Bilek, Ted; Jackson, Gerry L. 2004. Log sort yard economics, planning, and feasibility Gen. Tech. Rep. FPL-GTR-146. Madison, WI: U.S. Department of Agriculture, Forest Service, Forest Products Laboratory. 31 p.

A limited number of free copies of this publication are available to the public from the Forest Products Laboratory, One Gifford Pinchot Drive, Madison, WI 53726–2398. This publication is also available online at www.fpl.fs.fed.us. Laboratory publications are sent to hundreds of libraries in the United States and elsewhere.

The Forest Products Laboratory is maintained in cooperation with the University of Wisconsin.

About the Authors

John Rusty Dramm is a Forest Products Utilization Specialist in the Technology Marketing Unit of the Forest Products Laboratory, USDA Forest Service, in Madison, Wisconsin. Mr. Dramm's work focuses on potential applications of log sort yards to improve the viability of forestland restoration and fuels reduction activities. He also provides technical assistance in primary manufacturing conversion efficiency, quality, and productivity improvement of forest products. He has more than 20 years of industrial experience in wood products and aluminum manufacturing industries.

Dr. Robert Govett is a Professor in the College of Natural Resources at the University of Wisconsin in Stevens Point. Dr. Govett has more than 20 years experience in teaching, research, and extension activities, both in the western and Lake States regions of the United States and internationally. He has done considerable work in technical and financial feasibility studies for new forest products businesses, equipment replacement, and process and manufacturing improvement.

Dr. Ted Bilek spent 14 years at Canterbury University in Christchurch, New Zealand, doing research and teaching forestry economics and business-related courses. He is currently an economist at the Forest Products Laboratory, specializing in economic feasibility analysis.

Gerry Jackson is a Forest Products Marketing Specialist with the Technology Marketing Unit of the Forest Products Laboratory. Mr. Jackson provides marketing assistance to organizations engaged in rural community assistance and the forest products industry.

Acknowledgments

Coordination of log sort yard site visits was made possible by efforts of Federal and State utilization and marketing specialists throughout the United States. We especially recognize the efforts of Peter Lammert, Maine Department of Conservation; Dean Huber, USDA Forest Service, Northeastern Area; and Bill von Segen, USDA Forest Service, Region 6, State & Private Forestry. Several individuals, companies, and organizations contributed their insights into log sort yard operations, and we are most grateful for contributions from the following:

Roger Jaegel, Watershed Research and Training Center
Mark Stella, Rogue Institute
Terry Mace, Wisconsin Department of Natural Resources
Chris Edwards, Western Wood Products, Inc.
Bob McCarty, Weyerhaeuser Company
Marshall Peacore, Menominee Tribal Enterprises
Carl Henderson, Huber Resources Corporation
Bruce Edwards, E.D. Besse & Son
Peter Holman, Maxiwood
Jamie Barbour, Pacific Northwest Research Station, USDA Forest Service

Inch–pound unit	Conversion factor	SI unit
inch (in.)	25.4	millimeter (mm)
foot (ft)	0.3048	meter (m)
cubic foot (ft^3)	0.0283	cubic meters (m^3)
1 board foot	0.00236	cubic meters (m^3)
acre	0.4047	hectares (ha)

Contents

Log Sort Yard Economics, Planning, and Feasibility

John Rusty Dramm, Forest Products Utilization Specialist
State and Private Forestry, Forest Products Laboratory, Madison, Wisconsin

Robert Govett, Professor
University of Wisconsin–Stevens Point, Stevens Point, Wisconsin

Ted Bilek, Forest Products Economist
Forest Products Laboratory, Madison, Wisconsin

Gerry L. Jackson, Marketing Specialist
State and Private Forestry, Forest Products Laboratory, Madison, Wisconsin

Introduction

Log sort yards provide many benefits in the utilization and marketing of logs, wood, and fiber. Interest in commercial log sort yards has increased in the past decade in response to timber supply issues, changes in wood and fiber markets, and the need to recover more value from the available resource (Dramm and others 2002). In addition, forest-dependent rural communities, affected by changes in the timber supply situation, are searching for ways to build diversified and sustainable local forest products businesses.

Development of log sort yards could potentially provide better utilization and improve value recovery of small-diameter material and underutilized species. Log sort yards could also have application in forestland management by improving the utilization of wood and biomass removed from thinning operations and fuels reduction work.

This publication discusses basic marketing and economic concepts, planning approach, and feasibility methodology to assess log sort yard operations. Various options and procedures for determining sort yard feasibility are considered, and an example of the preliminary financial feasibility analysis methodology is provided. Application is pertinent to commercial, community, and government operated log sort yards.

Background

The USDA Forest Service is shifting its Federal forestland management strategies, calling for an increase in under-utilized mixed species and small-diameter material removals via thinning to accomplish forest management activities such as watershed restoration and forest fuels reduction. This is a major shift from past focus on larger-diameter sawtimber harvests on Federal timber sales. Dense, overstocked, small-diameter stands with heavy fuel loading require mechanical

treatment (e.g., thinning from below) and removal of excessive biomass, followed by prescribed burning to reduce these fuels, improve forest vigor, and restore forest landscapes. Over the next several decades, Forest Service land management operations will produce measurable quantities of small-diameter material and biomass.

New and innovative approaches to forest management, forest fuels reduction, and land restoration require efficient land management tools. The management of overstocked stands is often prohibitively expensive. Given the buildup of excessive forest fuels in the West, the expanding high risk of catastrophic wildfires combined with high fire suppression costs have created an increasing demand on the USDA Forest Service.

Consequently, Federal land managers are looking for more economical ways to reduce forest fuel loading in the West and new ways to market low-value material from thinning operations, fuels reduction work, and watershed restoration projects. In the eastern United States, better markets for underutilized hardwoods are also needed to facilitate improved forest management of State and private forestlands. At the same time, rural communities, affected by reductions in Federal timber sales, continue to search for economic opportunities to recovery from the loss of tax revenues and jobs at local mills. Improved utilization and marketing of small-diameter material and underutilized species would help improve the economics of such forestry operations (Dramm 1999) and help sustain forest-dependent communities.

The log sort yard project investigated potential opportunities for using log sort yards to improve raw material supply and identified several misperceptions and barriers to successful operations (Dramm and Jackson 2000). Information provided could help sustain timber-dependent rural communities by improving the distribution of small quantities of logs for local businesses in support of diversifying rural community economies. The nation's forestlands would also benefit from improved markets for materials removed from thinning operations and fuels treatment projects.

Dramm and others (2002) reviewed current log-sort yard operations in North America and made several recommendations for efficient and economical operation. The authors visited and conducted interviews at 18 log-sort yard operations, ranging from commercial to community and nongovernment-operated yards. Related site visits included concentration and mill log yard operations and a processor that makes soil amendment products from log yard debris. Such site visits provided valuable insights into log sort yard design, operation, log procurement, and marketing. An extensive literature search uncovered additional sources of log sort yard information.

Problems in Perception

In their research, Dramm and others (2002) observed that log sort yard projects are often based on subjective opinion rather than objective investigation. This approach can quickly turn into a deep emotional attachment for the project as extensive effort, time, energy, and money are expended with little hope for success. Given the uncertainty of log sort yard viability, it is essential that serious consideration be given to the planned programming approach presented in this publication. This is especially important for yards that will potentially process small-diameter and other low-value logs from forest fuels reduction projects and forest restoration work where the economics are not favorable.

During the course of their investigation, the authors also found a limited understanding of the basic principles of efficient yard operation. Examples include poor log sort yard design, excessive log inventory and storage, and use of the wrong type of equipment for handling materials. In a *Review of Log Sort Yards*, Dramm and others (2002) address several barriers to efficient log sort yards and provide recommendations for improvement. Sinclair and Wellburn (1984) and Hampton (1981) provide in-depth discussions of efficient yard sort yard design and operation.

The basic concept and direct benefits of log merchandising are generally understood.[1] What is not so evident is how log merchandising relates to harvesting operations. While physical space may preclude sorting at the woods landing, or where low volume makes it unjustifiable to sort in the woods, a log sort yard would have operational and economic advantages (M. Peacore, personal communication, 1996).

---

[1] Merchandising involves bucking tree-length logs into short logs and sorting according to the highest end-use for each log produced (Williston 1988).

Along similar lines, the log sort yard can offer improved merchandising where bucking can more easily be accomplished physically compared with merchandising logs in the woods. Better merchandising decisions can also be achieved at a log sort yard by a log grader with a good understanding of log specifications and markets. Automated log merchandisers could further improve bucking decisions (see Fig. 6).

Log Cost/Value Relationship

Misperceptions of log sort yard viability and benefits come from a lack of understanding of the basic relationship of log cost and product value to log size (i.e., marginal log diameter). Sorting small-diameter logs is an economically questionable proposition. The smaller the log diameter, the less valuable the log becomes and the more expensive it is to process through the yard.

The Canadian experience described in this publication indicates that a high percentage of large-diameter high-value logs are needed in the log mix to be profitable (Ministry of Forests 1999).

Commercial log sort yards in the Pacific Northwest have found economical ways to merchandise and sort small-diameter material and recover higher value from pulpwood (Dramm and others 2002). Recent developments in mechanized log handling and merchandising have been shown to improve the economics of sorting small-diameter logs. How economical these systems perform through an entire business cycle is not currently known. The recent downturn in markets should give a good indication of the economic performance of automated log sorting systems.

Competitive or Complementary?

The authors also found a general lack of understanding of what can and cannot be realistically accomplished with a log sort yard. There is a general perception that log sort yards are competitive in nature—that log yards compete for timber sought by other forest products operations. In fact, log sort yards are most often complementary to consuming mills, offering improved log procurement with a desirable log mix. Several independent commercial log sort yards provide services for larger integrated firms to recover a higher dollar return by sorting logs for highest end use. This is quite the opposite of the common perception of log sort yards as competitive in nature.

Log Sort Yard Benefits

Not surprising are the misperceptions of the direct and indirect benefits of log sort yards and several possible applications. Many misperceptions of direct benefits come from a lack of understanding of the basic principles of log sort yard operational efficiency (Dramm and others 2002). This includes the assumed viability of sorting low-value, small-diameter logs, which in reality poses a very difficult problem. The potential indirect benefits to improving local economic, social, and environmental qualities are equally not well understood. These are basic opportunity cost-type questions that deserve further consideration.

Community and Government Yards

Community and government operated log sort yards may provide opportunities for economic diversification for rural communities (Wallowa Resources 1997) while improving the economics of forestland management activities associated with overstocked, small-diameter stands in the West. Community and government log sort yards as well as commercial yards are being explored toward this end. Such yards are well intentioned, with objectives like providing small quantities of logs to local small businesses or providing better opportunities for improved forest management, fuels reduction, and restoration work through marketing of small-diameter material. Some objectives focus on intangibles like social and environmental benefits.

Although commercial log sort yards have a proven track record throughout North America, community and government log yards have had limited success. Several community log sort yards have been established, yet few have survived beyond 5 years. Government yards have been tried in the past, but none is known to exist today in the United States.

Failure of community and government yards is often due to poor management, lack of good business planning, deficiency in one or more critical factors related to resource supply, log markets, financial feasibility and performance, or lack of business "know-how". The authors' investigation indicates that a major specific cause of failure of community log sort yards is a lack of sufficient and consistent log supply. Other primary causes of failure are lack of hands-on business experience in running a log yard, rapid expansion into value-added operations (i.e., trying to do it all from the very beginning), and lack of objective planning and analysis of potential log sort yards. Secondary causes of failure include insufficient markets and market prices for lower grade logs.

The authors recommend that community log sort yards be operated as a business, such as a cooperative or corporation owned by the community. Government yards should operate in a similar business-like manner and require modifications to business accounting and financial reporting methods (Ministry of Forests 1999). For both types of yards, serious consideration must be given to employing an experienced log sort yard contractor to operate and manage day-to-day operations. The authors do not recommend that a community, nonprofit organization, or government agency try to run the yard. Operating a log sort yard requires experience in several disciplines, such as log procurement, log markets, manufacturing systems, industrial safety, and business management.

Success of both government and community log sort yard operations has been documented in Canada. Examples include the Vernon log yard in British Columbia (Wallowa Resources 1997, Ministry of Forests 1999) and the log sort yard of the Revelstoke Community Forestry Corporation (RCFC 2003). Innovative log sort yards, such as Vernon and Revelstoke, show that government and community log sort yards can realize higher values for the available timber resource and be self-sufficient when lumber markets are strong (Ministry of Forests 1999, RCFC 2003). Successful Canadian government and community log sort yards could serve as models for similar operations in the United States.

Vernon BC Government Log Yard

The Vernon log sort and sales yard operates under the auspices of the small-business timber program through the Ministry of Forests in British Columbia. Success is due in part to the employment of an experienced log sort yard operator under contract with the Ministry of Forests. The log yard contractor provides the labor, equipment, and experience necessary to run the yard. Tom Milne, Log Yard Manager, is a government employee who oversees operations, accounting, bid preparations, and contracts. The Ministry of Forests also maintains ownership of logs, which are harvested from Provincial forestlands and hauled to the Vernon yard under separate contracts (Ministry of Forests 1999). Log sales are conducted weekly by competitive sealed bid. Successful bidders have 1 week to pay for their logs and 2 weeks to remove them from the yard.

The Vernon log yard experience indicates that a primary key to financial success of community and government log sort yards is the ability to sell a fairly high percentage of large-diameter high-value premium logs (Ministry of Forests 1999). Log sort yard financial studies confirm that a supply of premium high margin logs is vital to financial success of a private log sort yard (Majestic Forest Management 1997). Financial success is directly related to the proportion of higher value premium logs that produce the greatest net profit margin. With a high enough percentage of logs with the greatest dollar margins, a log sort yard could operate successfully on perhaps 2 million cubic feet of softwood logs annually (Majestic Forest Management 1997).

Profitability of log sort yards is also directly linked to fluctuations in log market prices (Ministry of Forests 1999). The poorer the market, the higher the percentage of premium logs need to be sold for the yard to remain economically viable. About 75% of the logs sold at the Vernon yard are sawlogs and higher valued log products like veneer peeler blocks and house logs. The Vernon log yard project determined that it is not economical to sort pulpwood in the yard. Therefore, pulpwood is presorted at the landing, sold, and transported directly to a pulp mill. Given the desire to process small-diameter material through log sort yards in the western United States, this research finding has serious negative implications for projects focused solely on sort yards for small-diameter logs. Poorer markets also reduce the distance logs can be transported economically from the yard to consuming mills.

Revelstoke Community Log Yard

Other efforts, such as in Revelstoke, British Columbia, are investigating community-owned log sort yards (RCFC 2003). The Revelstoke community, in partnership with three local sawmills, purchased a tree farm license (TFL) to manage approximately 300,000 acres of Provincial forestland. The TFL is a Canadian system for public/private partnerships for multiple-use forest management of public lands. A company, or in this case the City of Revelstoke, purchases a TFL to manage public lands in exchange for timber removal rights.

The community's goal is to enhance local economic, social, and environmental qualities. A land use plan for Revelstoke's TFL was developed. To manage the TFL, the RCFC was formed by the city, which owns all shares in the RCFC.

Under Revelstoke's TFL, the annual allowable cut is approximately 3.5 million ft^3. Logs come from timber stand improvement operations (e.g., commercial thinning) in addition to timber harvests. Half the annual harvest allotted to timber removal rights is split among each of the three partner mills. The other half is allocated to the city and is sold on a competitive bid basis through the community yard. RCFC developed and operates the community log sort yard.

Products sold at the Revelstoke sort yard include a variety of high-valued log products, including softwood peelers (veneer logs), house logs, sawlogs, cedar shake blocks (for wood shingles), cedar poles, and spruce tonewood (music wood). Prices received for logs vary by species and grade, ranging from Canadian \$58 to \$250/m^3 (US\$1.10 to \$4.70 /ft^3). The RCFC log sort yard has generated dividends for Revelstoke for most years of operation. As with the government-operated Vernon log yard, low-valued, small-diameter material is presorted at the landing and transported directly to pulpwood markets to keep log-sorting costs down at the yard. These findings underscore some negative implications for small-diameter log sort yard operations.

Benefits of Community and Government Yards

Potential benefits of community and government log sort yards can include the economic stability of forest-dependent communities in the United States. For instance, in the private sector, bidding on Federal timber sales is a risky proposition that ties up a company's financial resources. Litigation over a Federal timber sale can run the course of several years (see section on lost opportunities resulting from lengthy litigation).

In contrast, with log sort yards sales, the successful bidder generally pays and takes possession of logs in just a few weeks, offering substantial cost savings and reduced financial risk. Coupled with a consistent supply of logs through the log sort yard, such benefits to wood-using businesses would encourage economic stability (Ministry of Forests 1999).

It is also logical to assume that this approach would result in a greater return to the government, with higher net prices paid for logs at the log yard compared with that associated with the traditional Federal timber sale. This is an opportunity cost problem that deserves more attention. The simple fact that a company will lower its risk by procuring logs from a sort yard rather than from Federal timber sales in itself should encourage higher dollar returns to the government.

However, the Canadian experience does not necessarily support the assumption of greater returns through log sort yards sales. The assumption holds up well when forest product markets are strong, but the opposite is true when markets fall (Ministry of Forests 1999). Other intangibles, such as social and environmental benefits, might also be expected (RCFC 2003). Again, the Canadian experience does not necessarily support these anticipated intangible benefits (Ministry of Forests 1999).

Forest Service Policy and Operational Changes

Several operational, policy, and judicial issues would need to be resolved for government and community operated log sort yards to operate successfully in the United States. For example, because small-diameter timber has low overall net value, the raw material supply from forest fuels reduction and land restoration projects may have to be supplemented with higher quality logs from timber sales program. Even then, some sort of subsidy would most likely be needed to defray the excessive cost of removing small-diameter material through fuels reduction and restoration efforts (see Subsidizing Uneconomical Log Sort Yards).

Changes to several policies would be critical in adapting log sort yards to improve forest and land management options. Some examples include the following:

- USDA Forest Service contracting and timber sale authorities, such as Stewardship Contracting authorities

- Federal log chain of custody requirements for tracking low-value, small-diameter, and underutilized material from Federal forests

- Forest Service policies for providing a consistent supply of material to log sort yards

To date, these policy issues have not been identified or studied.

Subsidizing Uneconomical Log Sort Yards

The issue of uneconomical log sort yards is an interesting one. The authors discourage long-term financial support for log sort yards, such as through grants, and recommend a viable self-sufficient business approach to establishing a yard. However, subsidies to defray the excessive cost of logs and other biomass to be processed may be in order. A subsidy may be a small price to pay, considering the alternative of expensive forestry operations such as thinning from below, forest fuels reduction, and fire suppression.

It may make sound economical sense to supply such negative-valued material if the potential cost of leaving it in the forest were greater than the cost of removing it; for example, the excessively high cost of fire suppression and ecological and property damage if such material is burned.

What really drives a log sort yard operation to being uneconomical, assuming it is reasonably well managed, is the high cost of the incoming log resource in comparison with the relatively low value of the products (see Economics). This concept is not well grasped by those who assume that standing small-diameter timber is worth some arbitrary value.

Although small-diameter material may have a positive gross value, its net value is often negative. In business accounting terms, this is called an absolute profit loss, where the value of a product does not even cover the cost to produce the product, never mind fixed costs like overhead or interest charges on working capital. In many cases, material from small-diameter thinning operations costs substantially more than the value of potential products that could be produced from it (D. Lynch, USDA Forest Service, Region 2, personal communication, 1999). The net value is negative, given the size, quality, harvesting and hauling costs, potential types of products from the logs, and available markets.

Where appropriate, the need for a subsidy in these circumstances might be eliminated if there is a negative cost associated with the standing timber that supplies the log sort yard. Note that this should not be confused with a subsidy to the sort yard—rather it is an accurate reflection of valuation of less than worthless (i.e., negative net value) raw material. This negative value should not be passed onto the log sort yard. Rather, log market forces should be the basis upon which valuation of incoming logs is made. This follows standard timber valuation practices for National Forest System (USDA Forest Service) timber sales. A variation of subsidizing small-diameter material would be to supplement the raw material supply of the log sort yard with higher valued, large-diameter logs from timber sales, as is common in the Vernon log sort yard in Canada.

Results of Lengthy Litigation

Lengthy litigation regarding fuels reduction, land restoration, timber stand improvement, and timber harvest must have resolution. The lengthy process is a concern for pressing resource issues like forest fuels reduction to curb the growing risk of catastrophic wildfire. For instance, delay in salvaging insect-killed timber often leaves a potentially valuable resource unusable because of rapid decline in quality. Here, lengthy litigation results in poor conservation and use of forest products resources, which often become an expensive liability.

Federal timber sale litigation also encourages alternative log procurement strategies employed by industry. This has resulted in a substantial increase in harvest pressure on State, county, industrial, and private lands with the reduction in Federal timber harvest levels. Litigation also encourages procurement of foreign logs such as radiata pine (*Pinus radiata*, D. Don) from countries like Chile and New Zealand.

There are also sanitary issues regarding the importation of foreign organisms on logs—a risk that is not incurred with domestic logs. Finally, there is an issue of "freshness." Logs from a local sort yard should be fresher than imported logs, which may have implications for processing. It should also mean less opportunity for decay or degrade to have occurred.

To some extent, litigation issues could work to the advantage of log sort yards in the United States. Logs purchased outright at yards would eliminate the costly litigation delays common to Federal timber sales. Other advantages, such as reduced time between bidding (for log stumpage) to time of possession, can reduce the risks of securing timber/logs from several years to just a few weeks. This can be especially important in volatile wood product markets. Additional disadvantages, such as the posting of timber sale performance bonds on Forest Service timber sales, are also overcome through log sort yards.

Economics

Dramm and others (2002) report that assuming a good supply of logs and markets, log sort yard economics are determined by

- log purchase costs as reflected by stumpage, harvest, and haul costs,

- log market prices FOB[2] log yard,

- per unit yard processing costs,

_____

[2] Free on board—the point where ownership and responsibility for transportation costs pass to the buyer.

- dollar value recovery of log products sold as a function of raw material cost, and

- log yard inventory cost and overhead charges.

Other considerations include the risk of catastrophic loss and risks associated with potential value loss resulting from factors like blue stain or insect attack and with wood product market fluctuations.

Log Cost/Value Relationships

The economic problem of forest products utilization and marketing, including log sort yards, centers on dealing with marginal logs (Hallock 1964, Barbour 1999). Marginal logs are characterized by low product value in comparison to log cost. Examples include small-diameter material, underutilized species, and poor quality logs. In any forest products venture, it is crucial to identify the diameter breakpoint of marginality where log product per unit value equals the total cost of processing that log.

For example, in relation to sawlog diameter, per unit (volume) sawlog cost decreases with increasing log diameter size to a point and then begins to increase (Fig. 1). The low point on the cost curve represents the sawlog diameter range where logs are processed most efficiently by the operation. Logs smaller or greater than this diameter range are more expensive to process.

Value increases with an increase in sawlog size (Fig. 2). Initially, value gradually increases to a point; value then rapidly increases as log diameter reaches high-value uses such as premium sawlogs.

The intersection of the cost curve with the product value curve defines the line of marginality (Fig. 3). This represents the average diameter where log product value equals log cost. Log diameters below this line result in higher costs than the value of the log, hence submarginal. One might conclude that submarginal logs should never be purchased or processed because cost is greater than log value. In reality, all forest products operations to some extent process a mixture of logs from both sides of the line of marginality. What is important is that operators process logs better than the average marginal log, taking into account a reasonable profit margin; otherwise, the venture is not economically viable.

The continuing overall trend toward smaller and poorer quality logs means managing marginal logs. One solution to the marginal log for operators is to improve log product mix procured by reducing the number of marginal logs purchased. This is precisely what the government-operated Vernon log yard does—only higher valued logs are processed in the yard (Ministry of Forests 1999). Small-diameter material (i.e., pulpwood) is not brought to the Vernon log yard for sorting. Instead, pulpwood is presorted from the higher-grade logs at the landing (i.e., the log loading area at the timber harvesting site) and transported directly to local

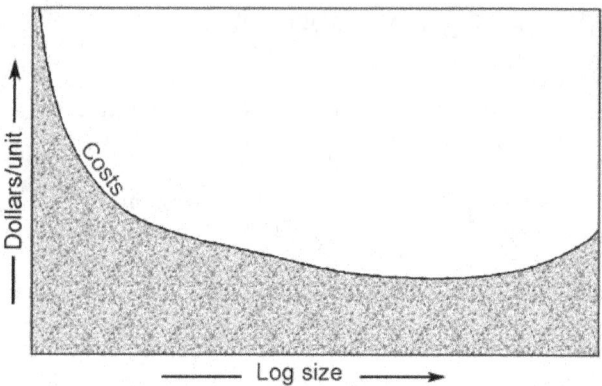

Figure 1—Cost curve showing relative sawlogs costs (i.e., stumpage, harvest, haul, and processing costs) in relation to sawlog diameter.

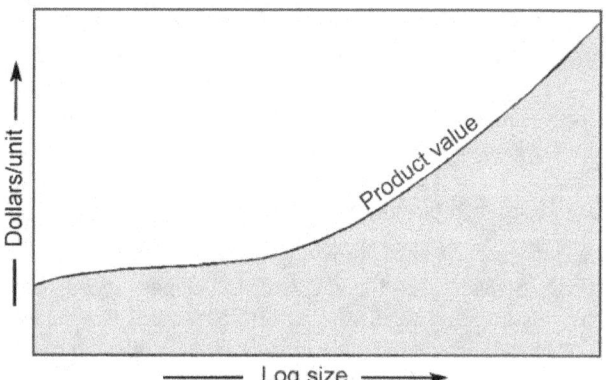

Figure 2—Product value curve showing relative potential value of products from sawlogs in relation to sawlog diameter.

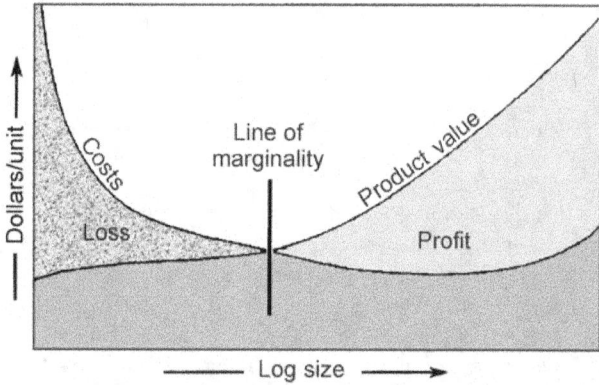

Figure 3—Concept of marginality. Marginal sawlog size is at the intersection of the cost curve with the product value curve. Here, product value equals log costs. Sawlogs smaller than the line of marginality or submarginal logs cost more than their potential value.

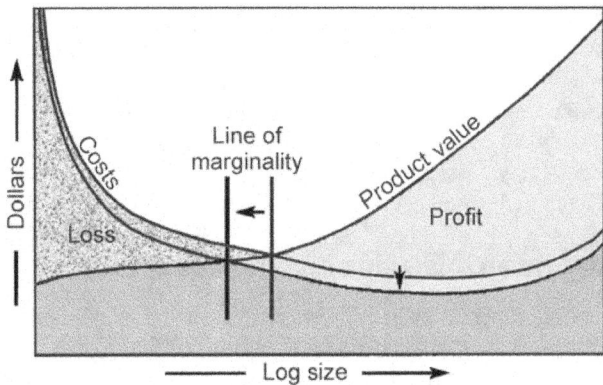

Figure 4—Lowering the cost curve decreases the marginal log size, allowing for better utilization of smaller logs.

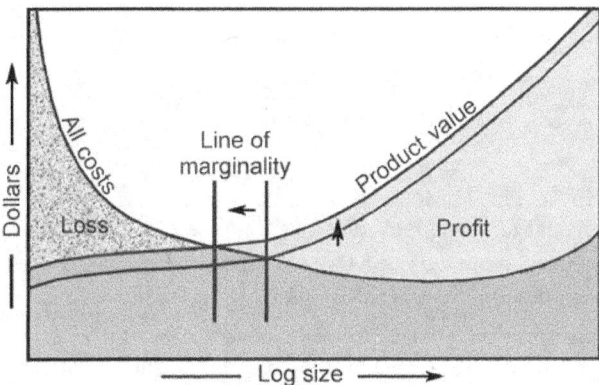

Figure 5—Raising the value curve also decreases the marginal log diameter.

pulp mills. This greatly reduces the material handling costs of low-grade logs and improves the average value of the logs brought to the yard.

Another option is to find ways to move the line of marginality (Fig. 3) to the left to be able to use smaller log size and lower log quality/value. This is accomplished by lowering the cost curve (Fig. 4), raising the value curve (Fig. 5), or a combination of both.

Lowering the Cost Curve

Several things can be done to lower the cost curve for the log sort yard (Fig. 4):

- Use an efficient yard layout and sorting systems design

- Handle and process (grade, scale, sort, load, transport) logs efficiently

  o Minimize log handling (number of times a log is picked up, transported, and set down)

- Transport logs in bunches (full loads) using full capacity of handling equipment

- Minimize effort in processing low-value logs

  o Process low-value logs in bunches rather than individually

  o Incorporate weight scaling truck loads instead of stick scale individual small low-value logs

- Match materials handling machine capability to volume, piece count, and weight of logs processed

  o Use proper log handling equipment for efficient processing to reduce overall cost and improve yard productivity

  o Do not over-design log handling equipment (i.e., use more expensive, higher capacity equipment than required)

  o Do not under-design log handling equipment or use the wrong piece of equipment, such as a forklift or skid steer loader to do the job of a more efficient front end loader

Special considerations for medium to large yards

- Employ small-log hand log handling and processing equipment (e.g., log sorting tables, linear sorting systems, log merchandisers)

- Use specialized equipment for each yard function (i.e., load, scale, grade, sort, transport, reload)

- Reduce long-term rolling stock maintenance cost and improve overall productivity of transport machines by paving log yard with asphalt

Special considerations for small yards

- Minimize log sort yard construction costs by using a former mill or other previously developed industrial site

- Purchase used materials-handling equipment in good condition at substantial savings over new equipment

- Use general purpose machines (e.g., medium capacity front-end loader) for all transporting, sorting, and loading rather than specialized machines for each function

Raising the Value Curve

In a similar manner, several things can be done to raise the value curve (Fig. 5):

- Improve log marketing by finding better markets and prices for sorted logs

- Improve log product mix brought for processing

- Incorporate log quality control program

  o Ensure conformance to log specifications for available markets

  o Produce accurate log lengths (e.g., trim log appropriately, reduce overlength, reduce log length variation)

  o Reduce number of mis-manufactured logs and control log damage

- Increase volume production of higher grade logs by proper bucking (i.e., log merchandising)

- Improve log merchandising with computer-optimized bucking solutions (large-scale log sort yard)

- Increase effort in processing high value logs to recover optimum value; emphasize quality over production

  o Use stick scaling of individual logs instead of weight scaling of log truck loads

  o Identify logs by plastic tags to improve inventory control and log chain of custody

  o Make extra effort to reduce log handling damage

  o End coat veneer logs to prevent end checks and splits

- Incorporate semi-processing (e.g., debarking and chipping logs and peeling poles)

- Employ a debarker and chipper to use short lengths from bucking operations

- Market firewood and other products from log sort yard residue and debris

- Upgrade high-quality sawlogs (e.g., buck high-quality hardwood logs to veneer lengths)

- Improve log bucking practices by training employees in principles of log grades related to log production

Planned Programming Approach

The authors recommend a planned programming approach to log sort yard development. This involves a step-by-step logical progression of several developmental stages (Sinclair and Wellburn 1984): (1) log sort yard feasibility and business planning; (2) siting, layout, design, and construction; and (3) operations and business management. Undertaking such a project requires knowledge of resource inventory and procurement, civil and industrial engineering principles, forest products marketing, business finance, supervision, and business management. This section covers the first steps in log sort yard planning and feasibility.

Planning aspects need to be considered during each phase of log sort yard development and eventual operation. This

suggests taking a systems approach to project development led by a project planning team of specialists that includes a wood procurement forester, logging/civil engineer, industrial engineer, forest products marketing specialist, and business management consultant. In addition, key personnel who will operate the yard should be part of the team. Business advisors include an accountant, investor, and attorney.

Purpose of Business Planning

The importance of business planning cannot be overemphasized. Most startup businesses fail within the first 5 years (Entrepreneur Magazine 1995). The business planning process points out weaknesses and deficiencies through market and financial feasibility analyses. Consequently, a properly developed business plan improves the chances for success. Howe and Bratkovich (1995) provide an excellent step-by-step guide for planning wood products businesses.

Business planning accomplishes four basic things:

1. Planning forces the team to think strategically and take a critical objective look at starting or expanding the business (Bangs 1995).

2. A formalized business plan provides a business owners' manual for developing and operating their business. It is a working roadmap to success (Bangs 1995).

3. A business plan is essential to obtain financing. It provides the lender with a basis to evaluate venture startup or expansion plans. The business plan communicates to others the value of the new enterprise (Bangs 1995).

4. The rigorous process of business planning improves the likelihood of success by identifying difficulties, risks, problems, and strategies to overcome barriers or abandon enterprises where problems cannot be overcome, thereby saving time, energy, and money (Govett 2001).

Planning begins with feasibility studies to explore potential viable opportunities. Feasibility studies evaluate markets and financial aspects of the proposed operation. They help identify strengths, weaknesses, opportunities, and threats (SWAT Analysis) to the potential log yard operation; assess risks; and carefully consider a number of critical factors for success. A formalized business plan[3] is developed for strategically guiding the business, identifying operational procedures, and securing financial backing. The detailed market feasibility and financial analyses, risk assessment, and supporting documentation are included as appendices to the business plan.

---

[3] In the context of this paper, the business plan takes on a broader meaning than described by some traditional definitions and includes strategic, marketing, and business operating plans.

The rigorous process of developing a business plan involves considerable work in identifying likely difficulties, hurdles to be overcome, and risks. This process requires that those who proceed with the plan—bring the business to fruition and then execute it—have rigorously considered the overall environment. It is frequently the case that in the development of the business plan, problems or hurdles that cannot be overcome are identified and the enterprise can be abandoned before financial losses have accrued. In contrast, starting a business with less research and being unaware of problems can lead to failure, often at great cost. The use of the business plan reduces the risk of failure where an incorrect decision to proceed is rejected in the planning process.

Planning Team

The log sort yard planning team gathers resource and market information prior to making a feasibility analysis. Planning a log sort yard requires knowledge in many areas, such as log yard design, construction, and operations as well as project and financial management. Timber resource assessment, log procurement, log handling equipment requirements, log grading and specifications, and marketing knowledge need to be covered (Mater Engineering 1998).

The planning team should consist of those who will design, construct, and operate the log sort yard (Sinclair and Wellburn 1984). The team should be responsible for developing and analyzing potential options and choosing a workable plan to meet the proposed goals and objectives of the log sort yard. Professional assistance (e.g., accountant, procurement forester, consulting engineer, attorney, forest products marketing specialist, banker) will be required at various stages of planning. The log sort yard supervisor and yard foreman should be included in the planning team.

Govett (2001) recommends that a generalist head the planning team and lead the planning process. Specialists tend to lose interest outside their area of expertise and too often attempt to redefine issues in terms of their expertise. Additional suggestions include the following:

- Beware of becoming emotionally attached to a project analysis or of advice from anyone who has become emotionally attached to the analysis. Beware of project cheerleaders who will not give up on a bad idea.

- Beware of placing too much weight on advice from experts on the fringe of their expertise—watch out for phrases like "I'm not an expert in this area, but…"

- Beware of placing too much weight on the advice of experts who have something to gain or lose as a result of selection of alternative courses of action (e.g., equipment vendor).

- Beware of placing too much weight on industry averages, general rules of thumb, or past experience.

- Justify your assumptions; the most important question is "Why this assumption?"

Knowledgeable members of the planning team should be able to set the main objective of the log sort yard and handle the preliminary financial feasibility analysis of options, as well as the assessment of initial resource supply, log markets, and log sort yard site evaluation. Log sort yard planning and determining the feasibility of alternatives is a screening process that evaluates the available raw material, potential products, markets and industrial infrastructure, and financial analysis. Potentially viable scenarios are constrained by technical, economic, and market limitations. Finding feasible log sort yard opportunities is an elimination process, filtering through each of these constraints. Technical constraints limit the types of products possible from the available resource supply. Available markets further refine suitable product options. Financial analysis determines which (if any) marketable products will generate sufficient revenue to justify a log sort yard operation.

Log Sort Yard Objectives

One of the first duties of the planning team is to define the main objectives of the log sort yard—its purpose and how it might be achieved. This sets the stage for how the economics, planning, and feasibility of the log sort yard are determined and ultimately how a yard is operated.

Several main objectives could be considered in the development and use of log sort yards. Traditionally, these objectives include the following:

- For-profit independent operation or profit center of a larger integrated forest products company

- Cost savings center

- Risk reduction

- Multiple objectives (combination of previous objectives)

- Improved economics of forest management

For-Profit Yards

Most commercial log sort yards are in business to make a profit. Profit should be the main driving force behind all for-profit business investments. For-profit log yards are in the business of making money, not sorting logs. The independent log sort yard, with the goal of producing a profit, needs to have returns on investment greater than that on other investments with similar risk. Otherwise, there is no real financial reason to invest in a log sort yard venture. In for-profit operations, each log sort is scrutinized for its contribution to profit and is consequently governed by the law of diminishing returns. Similarly, a log sort yard within an integrated forest products company may operate as a profit center.

The only time a for-profit business (or profit center) should invest outside this rule is to meet regulatory laws such as those related to safety, health, and environmental regulations. Even then, these are factored into the overall profit margin calculation. An example of this is the practice of using three or more log grading and scaling bays to decouple operations, which separates the log graders, scalers, and yard workers from mobile equipment in the yard for safety reasons (Sinclair and Wellburn 1984).

Cost Savings

Integrated log sort yard operations (e.g., sort yards within a logging company or serving a large integrated forest products firm) may operate as a cost savings center rather than a profit center to the benefit of overall operations (Sinclair and Wellburn 1984). This will influence the financial analysis and justification to investors on how to improve the overall bottom line. Although a log yard may operate at a net loss, the benefits in an integrated operation may come in the form of a more desired log mix and overall bottom-line profitability for the company as a whole.

Risk Reduction

Large integrated forest products firms have another log yard objective. The benefits of risk reduction can be quantified and factored into the economic benefits. As an analogy, many forest products companies own or lease timberland. Often, timberland is not based on the return on investment, but rather on ensuring a supply of timber regardless of market. In terms of risk reduction, a log sort yard could provide another source of wood and fiber (i.e., diversified log procurement) to help even out log flow and inventories for an integrated forest products firm (Sinclair and Wellburn 1984). In both cases, these types of internal subsidies are not quantified financially, but they are strategically important to the competitiveness of the firm.

Multiple Objectives

There are countless scenarios for applications of commercial log sort yards and implications of their objectives on log sort yard planning and justification. These scenarios often have multiple objectives. For example, in the 1990s, a downturn in market pulp prices encouraged independent log sort yards as well as integrated wood products operations to find better log markets for pulpwood (i.e., small-diameter softwood stems). The objective of a log sort yard in this case was to capture higher log value by sorting sawlog, veneer peelers, and stud blocks from the general mix of logs from pulpwood timber sales and thinning operations. Such value-added contributed to overall profitability while finding markets to move wood and fiber, thereby reducing excess wood inventories (i.e., cost savings by reducing log inventories) (C. Edwards, Western Wood Products, Eugene, Oregon, personal communication, 1999). Other examples include log concentration yards where cost savings (achieved by concentrating loads for highway tractor–trailer log trucks or

by railcar) are coupled with risk reduction by diversifying log supply from small independent timber producers.

Improved Economics of Forest Management

Opportunities for log sort yards to improve forest management are also worth considering. In many respects, this is similar to the objectives of cost savings and risk reduction, but here the log sort yard operates to benefit forest health while stimulating the rural economy. Log sort yards may be beneficial in improving the removal and economical use of small-diameter material from fuels reduction and restoration projects in the West. Even then, such log sort yard operations may not be economically viable without some sort of subsidy because of the high costs of delivered raw material, low value of the material, and lack of ready markets (see Subsidizing Uneconomical Log Sort Yards).

Feasibility Analysis

Preliminary Feasibility

Considerable time and energy are often expended in exploring new business start-ups and expansion projects by gathering data and refining assumptions, only to find that the project is unfeasible even under best-case assumptions. Attention should then be focused elsewhere. Not surprisingly, this conclusion becomes more difficult to the extent that individuals form an emotional attachment to the idea after expending considerable effort, time, and money. This all too common situation underscores the need for a better way to help focus on more promising opportunities. A better approach is to begin with a simple preliminary financial feasibility analysis using reasonable best-case assumptions that can be relatively easy to estimate.

Preliminary development of financial feasibility should begin early in the planning process. Preliminary financial analysis avoids wasting time and energy. It helps to bring focus on the big picture, to identify critical data needs and assumptions, and to narrow potential opportunities. Preliminary financial analysis can help depersonalize feasibility analysis so that decisions are made on an objective rather than subjective basis, which helps to prevent emotional attachment to a poor investment. Preliminary financial analysis also converts passive discussion into action and illuminates opportunities and problems.

Preliminary financial feasibility should start with best-case scenarios for each option under consideration. Various log-sorting scenarios can be quickly and easily analyzed to narrow potential opportunities. Analysis identifies those options worthy of further consideration. Such simple preliminary feasibility studies quickly demonstrate projects that are not worth pursuing further. Determining preliminary financial and technical feasibility reduces the time and effort spent on evaluating nonviable options and helps focus attention on critical information needs.

In doing the preliminary feasibility, it is usually best to start with a simplified financial analysis, then complicate and compound as necessary. Focus efforts on discovering the critical variables. Do not spend time on complicating and compounding the trivial.

Always ask why you are using each assumption and justify your logic behind each. Raw material resource, products, markets, costs, prices, and other assumptions used in feasibility analysis are critically important.

If the results of preliminary financial analysis look at least marginal or better, the option is probably worth investigating further. Any options that do not look promising under best-case scenarios should be dropped. When options have been narrowed to perhaps three to five, a detailed analysis of raw material supply, products and markets, processing, and financial aspects of the project can be done.

In some cases, the preliminary financial analysis may indicate that the original concept is flawed or otherwise unworkable. However, a more appropriate dimension of undertaking may be identified as a result of interactive discussion in doing the analysis and more broadly considering problems and opportunities.

Given the vast differences among log sort yards and the uncertainty of favorable economics, issues regarding revenue from log sorting and associated costs to determine gross margins must be considered on a case-by-case basis. Log sorting studies conducted with a representative batch of unsorted logs are a simple and effective way of collecting data for the preliminary feasibility analysis. Simple spreadsheet programs, such as LOGYARDFEAS.xls, analyze study data and separate the potentially economical sorting options from nonviable options (see Appendix A).

Example

In the following text, we present an example of a preliminary financial analysis. This analysis is based on theoretical assumptions and should not be used as a likely scenario.

Example log input data are shown in Table 1. Log procurement cost ($/unit) is the cost of logs delivered to the yard and includes stumpage, harvest, and haul costs. A reasonable estimate of the actual log sorting cost ($/unit) of logs processed through the yard is used in this example. These include the variable costs associated with loading and unloading, grading and scaling, sorting, and storage of logs. In this hypothetical case, sorting costs for ponderosa pine and Douglas-fir are about the same. Pulpwood and woods run[4] logs are more expensive to sort as a result of their smaller

average diameter (i.e., higher number of pieces per unit volume). Log scale (unit volume) is the volume for each log species/grade of logs delivered to the yard, such as might be determined by a log sorting study or timber resource supply analysis. Units may be any measure of log volume or weight such as cubic feet or cubic meters, board foot log scale, cords, cunits ($100 \text{ ft}^3 = 1$ cunit), or tons.

An example of log product output data is shown in Table 2, which shows log use sort/product category, associated log market selling price per unit, and unit volume by each log species/grade classification (from Table 1). Log market selling prices[5] for various products produced at the yard are determined by surveys of potential customers. Surveys are typically conducted by contacting local mills and other wood-using businesses that would be interested in the logs available. A breakdown of sorted log products can be estimated if the potential log product from the incoming log resource is well known. Otherwise, a simple log sorting yield study can be conducted to determine the breakdown of log products from each log species/grade classification (Table 1). Table 3 shows an example summary of preliminary log sort yard feasibility.

Interpretation of Gross Margin

The final calculation of gross margin (Table 3) will be of greatest interest and importance to the planning team. Examining the gross margin on a cost/unit basis by each log species/grade classification directly indicates the dollars that remain after log procurement and sorting costs are covered. A positive gross margin indicates a scenario worth further investigation and intensive financial analysis. A negative gross margin indicates a nonviable scenario that is not worth further investigation.

In the example summary (Table 3), Douglas-fir shows the greatest gross margin at $98.19/unit, followed by ponderosa pine at $46.74/unit and woods run at $31.13/unit. These log species/grade categories are worthy of further study. Pulpwood, however, shows a negative gross margin of −$3.89/unit. Even under the assumed best-case scenario, this hypothetical example indicates that pulpwood is not economically viable. In this hypothetical example, no matter what other assumptions are used, pulpwood cannot be an economically viable option. Thus, this option is eliminated from further study. Again, the preliminary analysis will save considerable effort, time, and money spent chasing poor investment scenarios and help bring focus on more promising opportunities.

---

[4] Woods run logs are purchased logs (average log price) that have not been graded or presorted; also known as camp run.

[5] Log selling price at the yard (or valuation in the case of integrated companies).

Table 1—Example log input data for various species and grades

Species or grade	Log procurement cost ($/unit)	Log sorting cost ($/unit)	Log scale (unit volume)
Ponderosa pine	300	60	720
Douglas-fir	320	65	2,760
Pulpwood	75	95	1,980
Woods run	180	75	5,240

Table 2—Example log product output data for various products

Log use sort/product category[a]	Log market selling price ($/unit)	Pine (unit)	Douglas-fir (unit)	Pulpwood (unit)	Woods run (unit)
Peeler blocks	950	—	160	—	—
Pine sawlog	650	130	—	—	80
DF sawlog	600	—	290	—	410
DF stud bolts	500	—	1,985	480	2,090
Poles	400	520	—	—	—
Pulpwood	60	—	245	1,480	2,600
Firewood	5	70	80	20	—
Total (output)		720	2,760	1,980	5,240

[a]DF is Douglas-fir.

Table 3—Example summary of preliminary log sort yard feasibility

Species or grade	Average log value[a] ($/unit)	Gross margin[b] ($/unit)
Ponderosa pine	406.74	46.74
Douglas-fir	483.19	98.19
Pulpwood	166.11	-3.89
Woods run	286.13	31.13

[a]Average value of logs in test (calculated from Table 2).
[b]Log value minus log procurement and sorting costs.

This example illustrates that what log sort yard planners and managers really need is an effective and simple way to simultaneously consider both log sort yard revenue and costs. The gross margin is used to identify both those species of logs and grades within species that offer the greatest potential for economic return, as well as those that pose the greatest problems, risk of losses, or unacceptably low margin returns.

Armed with this kind of information, log sort yard planners are in a position to begin an in-depth study of log sort yard feasibility, problems, and possible solutions. In some cases, the problem may simply be that the delivered log price is too high relative to the volume of logs processed, the mix of log products (output), and the log selling price realized.

Other Uses for Preliminary Feasibility Analysis

The testing of different combinations of log sorts (number of sorts and types of log products) can be used to help identify an optimal mix of log procurement and markets to best meet the financial objectives of the yard. It is entirely possible that a yard is profitable overall, but it is essentially making nothing or actually losing money on some log species or grades. Identification and understanding of such problems are always the first step towards solution. Consequently, it is crucial to identify marginal log products and minimum log diameter breakpoints. The preliminary financial feasibility methodology can be applied to the problem of profit contribution for each individual log sort. It helps establish the number of log sorts, log sort markets, and profit contribution from each log sort.

In addition, preliminary feasibility methodology can be used to evaluate log procurement and log product prices. The spreadsheet can provide a quick look at how much the price of a given grade of log would have to be reduced for that grade to yield an acceptable gross margin. This is easily done on an iterative trial and error basis. In similar fashion, sensitivity analysis can be conducted to test the effects of varying costs and revenues for identifying the variables most critical to the analysis.

Alternatives for Sorting Logs

Preliminary feasibility methodology can address another important issue: whether a log sort yard is the best option available to achieve desired objectives. The methodology can assess not only various log sort yard scenarios but also other alternatives for sorting logs, such as presorting low-valued logs (pulpwood and other small-diameter material) at the landing to reduce hauling costs and log sort yard handling and processing costs. In fact, alternatives to a log sort yard should be properly considered before deciding that a log sort yard is the best option to pursue. Dramm and others

(2002) discuss several possible options for sorting logs:

- Develop a log sort yard operation
- Sort logs at the landing
- Sort logs at a mill yard
- Develop a concentration yard operation
- Develop a satellite processing (e.g., chip mill) yard operation
- Do not sort logs
- Combinations of these options

Each option for economical log sorting has advantages and disadvantages, and each has an associated opportunity cost. Should a log sort yard be employed or is some other alternative more economical? Is it more economical to sort logs in a yard or at the landing? Are the additional costs of a log sort yard less than the net value gained by sorting? Is a traditional timber sale more economical? Is it more economical to treat excessive fuel loading biomass on site and not try to utilize any wood and fiber? These are all opportunity cost questions.

Information and Data Collection

The log sort yard planning team gathers resource and market information prior to making a feasibility analysis (Mater Engineering 1998). Knowledgeable members of the planning team should be able to handle initial resource supply, market, and site evaluation.

Resource Supply Data

An experienced consulting/professional forester should be retained to provide a detailed resource analysis. Data are collected by timber cruising at several typical sites. To accurately estimate log diameter and grade mix, timber cruise data should include tree size (diameter and merchantable height), tree grade distribution, and taper class. Data on resource supply and log market demand (Majestic Forest Management 1997) should include the following:

- Available timber supply—Current net timber inventory volume (i.e., net growth minus timber product output) and projected available log volume and future annual volumes.

- Species and log size distribution—Charts and graphs summarizing species and log size distributions; specific distribution data by supply location, species, and tree diameter.

- Log market demand—Current and future log volume demand by species and product (i.e., sawlogs, veneer logs, pulpwood) for each mill and wood products manufacturer; average and range of prices paid for each log product.

- Industry description—Description of the industry, which lists each mill, annual log consumption, and company contact; descriptions of major wood-using mills.

- Working circle map—Location of proposed log sort yard and distance from available timber resources (by volume) and log markets (by volume); log transportation corridors to and from the log sort yard.

- Market supply and demand—Listing of each potential product from targeted resource by species and volume; narrative description of timber supply match (i.e., timber supply to industrial capacity by products).

- Log costs (FOB log yard)—Average and range of stumpage prices and logging and haul costs FOB for log sort yard for targeted resource supply areas, by species and log product.

- Log production flow variation—Seasonal variation in log production; effects of spring breakup/mud season, winter logging, fires, and other restrictions.

- Forest inventory analysis (FIA)—Forest inventory and timber product output data from USDA Forest Service, Forest Inventory Analysis National Program. (Refer to Appendix B for contact information.)

Site Analysis

Large log sort yard projects require a detailed site analysis by a civil engineer (e.g., forest engineer or consulting engineer) prior to construction. On-site evaluation of potential log sort yard locations should consider (1) transportation and access to log sort yard, (2) distance from log supply, (3) distance to markets, (4) physical site features (e.g., surface material, slope, available acreage), (5) necessary site development, (6) required services and utilities, (7) land ownership, (8) permits and licensing requirements, and (9) environmental concerns (e.g., restrictions on stormwater surface runoff).

Labor Costs

Labor and operating costs are based on those costs specific to the area. These data are available from the State department of commerce and local chambers of commerce.

Utility and Service Hookups

Discussions with local utilities define necessary hookup and service charges for electric, telephone, waste disposal, water, and sewer services for the proposed log sort yard site.

Materials Handling and Equipment

Equipment manufacturers and vendors can supply data on machine specifications and performance; purchase price; operating, repair, and maintenance costs; machine reliability; and machine service life. In general, the simplest way to determine if a machine will satisfy the demands is to visit existing log sort yards. Visits to log sort yards or related operations (logging operations and mill log yards) are beneficial in refining the basic log yard equipment data supplied by manufactures and vendors. It is important to ask specific questions to establish the reliability of information.

Selection of proper handling and processing equipment is critical to log sort yard design. Selection of the correct size, type, and make of machines for the log sort yard has a significant impact on potential productivity and costs. In addition, the sorting system will have a major influence on the type and size of machines needed (Sinclair and Wellburn 1984). Log processing systems must match volume, log diameter, and distribution for the number of projected log use sorts. The log sort yard must be balanced with the appropriate piece production rate and volume anticipated.

The planning team needs to obtain information to establish machine performance and operating productivity. Log handling equipment is limited by its machine duty cycle and other operational characteristics. Machine productivity is controlled by the piece count production rate (Sinclair and Wellburn 1984). The volume of logs processed is a function of machine lifting capacity. Note that selected equipment also influences the physical layout of the log sort yard, such as the machine turning radius (see Processing under Critical Factors).

Log Market Data

A forest products marketing specialist should be employed to conduct the market analysis. Sources of marketing information (e.g., forest products primary and secondary industry directories) are available in several States. State departments of commerce, State foresters, and economic development councils are potential sources for wood industry contacts. General business directories can be found in the reference section of a public library. Small business development centers (SBDCs) and the Small Business Administration (SBA) can provide assistance in identifying potential customers. Contacts can also be obtained through interviews of managers of local forest products firms.

Several methods can be used to gather market information. Potential market and product pricing information can be obtained by telephone interviews and visits to wood products producers. Follow-up should include phone interviews of potential customers. Basic procurement, marketing, and operating information could include the following (Mater Engineering 1998):

- Interest in purchasing potential sorted log products

- Interest in purchasing pulpwood

- Interest in purchasing semi-processed log products (e.g., debarked stud logs, peeled posts and poles, clean pulp chips)

- Interest in purchasing products other than logs (e.g., grape stakes, tree stakes, corral and hop poles, clean chips, and bark mulch)

- FOB log sort yard and mill prices for log and allied products

- Available resource supply (volume and specifications by product category) to determine potential sales interest in purchasing logs from a sort yard

- Log sort yard siting concerns

- Competition for available timber resource

Critical Factors

There are seven critical factors to consider in planning a log sort yard (Dramm and others 2002; E. Davis, 1995, personal communication). Each log sorting option should be evaluated in relation to each critical factor. All the following factors are critical to successful log sort yard business ventures. Weakness in or the lack of one or more of these factors could lead to project failure. Considering each of these factors in logical order will define feasible options.

The following factors are generally used to evaluate opportunities for forest products economic development (Mater 1988; State of Wisconsin 1989; E. Davis, personal communication, 1995).

1. Raw material resource characterization and assessment

2. Potential product options from available resource

3. Market feasibility of potential product options

4. Processing technology requirements (e.g., piece count production rate) for handling and processing available raw material resource

5. Financial feasibility of log sort yard operation for available markets

6. Management team and other business considerations

7. Safety, health, and environmental regulations and licensing that could limit project success

The planning team brainstorms and categorizes each critical factor to develop a list of strengths, weaknesses, opportunities, and threats (SWAT analysis) for each sorting option and to further refine more promising options (Dramm and others 2002). In addition, the team conducts a risk analysis of possible factors that would be potentially catastrophic to the operation.

Raw Material Resource

Of primary interest to the forest products industry is the raw material supply, which includes resource inventory, availability, sufficient and consistent supply, stumpage price, harvesting and log transport costs, location in relation to manufacturing facilities, siting, transportation infrastructure, quality and quantity, and physical properties, as well as any unique attributes that can influence the product and its markets.

The first consideration in planning a log sort yard is the ability to secure the available resource supply. *Guarantee of a consistent timber supply is the major long-term, overriding issue for establishing and maintaining a viable forest products business* (Mater Engineering 1998), including log sort yard operations. This cannot be overstated. A primary objective of the log sort yard is to smooth out supply flow problems for log buyers and their mills by providing a more consistent supply of desired log mix.

For large yards, this means a good, consistent, and dependable long-term supply of logs in order to recoup investment costs. Smaller yards with minimal development costs can recover these costs over a shorter period. Uncertainty of timber supply creates difficulties. Planning should not be pursued until a secure and consistent raw material supply is determined. To calculate the potential available resource for the feasibility analysis, use half the available timber supply (i.e., net total annual growth – timber product output) (T. Mace, personal communication, 2001).

General timber supply information is often available from Federal and State forestry agencies or industrial forestland managers. Information on the available resource may not be detailed enough for an adequate assessment of raw material resource availability. When critical resource data are not available or lack sufficient detail, a professional consulting forester should be employed to gather the required information.

Resource supply information can have a substantial impact on the economic viability of a log sort yard facility, so it is important that it provide an accurate resource assessment. A forest description and typical timber supply should be provided in narrative form and summarized in a table (Majestic Forest Management 1997, Mater Engineering 1998). A map should be included that shows the working circle and its associated timber supply areas, consuming mills, and transportation corridors.

Resource information should include the following (Majestic Forest Management 1997):

- Targeted working circle and acreage for 5, 10, 15, and 20 years
- Summary of diameter class size, height, species mix, and number of trees per acre by
  o Specific resource supply location (e.g., targeted harvest/thinning/restoration sites)
  o Forest stand type
  o Forestland ownership

- Allowable annual cut (AAC) and actual harvest volumes for previous 5 to 10 years
- Timber product output (TPO) data within the working supply circle
  o List of consuming mills
  o Current mill/manufacturing capacity (e.g., volume and percentage of maximum capacity) for each mill
  o Log volume by log grade and product use class purchased by these mills
  o Source of log procurement inventories for each individual mill
- Excess log volumes available for purchase (i.e., volumes in excess of TPO)
- Available timber supply diameter class distribution for each timber stand type, site class, and ownership
  o Number of trees and volume per acre
  o Number of logs and volume per tree
  o Log quality (volume of logs by log grade)
  o (If possible) logging chance characteristics such as slope, access, and soils for each stand type
- Harvesting systems and costs (average and range) for typical stands and various stand treatments (e.g., timber harvest, commercial thinning, restoration work, forest fuels reduction)
- Timber stand improvement (TSI) and restoration project costs (average and range)
- Entry time of harvest/TSI by timber unit, landowner, and seasonal restrictions
- Rules, regulations, laws, court orders, and similar restrictions that affect future resource availability
- Other restrictions for harvest consideration, such as maximum diameter size

Critical to the detailed resource analysis is knowledge of log distribution by diameter and grade class and of volume by species that will be processed annually through the log yard. This is necessary to determine potential products, product prices, and log processing and handling equipment performance requirements (e.g., piece count rate and machine lifting capacity requirements) of the proposed log sort yard. A breakdown of products produced from the log resource by diameter class and species is also needed.

Volumes and market prices for each log product processed through the yard are used to determine profit contribution for each species, grade, diameter, and length class. This again is tied to the available resource. Specific raw material characterization is necessary to be able to determine suitable log products that could be made from the resource.

Timber cruise information on the available timber supply is needed from several typical forest sites to determine log grade and diameter distribution. This information should include species, tree diameter at breast height, volume per acre, volume per tree, number of logs per tree, log length and diameter, taper class, and tree grade distribution.

Products

When the available timber resource has been identified and raw material characterized, the next step is to determine what can be produced from the available raw material. A breakdown of products from the log resource by diameter class is needed. Product volumes and market prices for each product are used to determine profit contribution. In the early stages of a preliminary financial analysis, reasonable assumptions need to be made as to products produced and value per unit.

Raw material characterization is necessary to determine suitable products that could be made from the timber resource. Material properties of the available resource suggest potential products. Market trends for various products, existing product shortages, and new technological developments help further refine potential products. An important consideration is for the product to meet the end-use performance requirements expressed by log specifications. Careful consideration of product mix and differentiation (e.g., competitively priced, good quality) is crucial in today's markets.

General product options for logs include a full range of hardwood and softwood log quality, from no-value, small-diameter logs to high-value, large-diameter logs that yield high-quality factory lumber. Table 4 lists various types of log sort yard products.

Traditionally, large-diameter softwood logs have been sawn into high-value commodity appearance-grade products called factory lumber (e.g., primarily shop and industrial clear grades and moulding stock) and dimension lumber as well as veneer for plywood. Factory lumber is made into products like windowframe stock, cutstock and millwork, moulding, door sash, cabinets, and furniture. Larger logs offer a variety of quality levels, from low grade to premium sawlogs and softwood peeler blocks. In addition, large logs also yield commodity yard lumber for general construction purposes, including Select and Common boards and structural lumber (e.g., 2- by 4-in. studs).

The small softwood log resource provides a uniform resource of moderate quality. Small-diameter material is used for commodity yard lumber (i.e., dimension lumber and studs) as well as panels (e.g., oriented strandboard (OSB), waferboard, particleboard, medium density fiberboard), engineered wood products (e.g., I-joists, roof trusses), and pulp for papermaking. Although small-diameter logs offer

Table 4—Log sort yard products

Sawlogs, bolts, and blocks	Semi-processed log products	Specialty log products	Residuals from yard debris
Factory logs	Debarked stud logs	Burls	Firewood
Structural lumber logs	Clean pulp chips	Figured maple	Bark mulch
Stud logs/bolts	Peeled utility poles	Carving blocks	Colored chip mulch
Veneer logs	Fence posts and rails	Grape stakes	Biomass for energy
Peeler blocks	Export cants	Tree stakes	Hog fuel
Pulpwood	Landscape timbers	Orchard props	Wood pellets
Boltwood/fiber		Music wood	Rock/stone
Tie logs			Fines and mineral
Cabin bolts			
Construction logs			
Pallet logs			
House logs			
Utility logs			
Local use logs			

moderate quality, they have less overall potential value than that offered by large-diameter logs. The main problem associated with small-diameter logs is the occurrence of natural defects such as small knots.

Potential options for producing products from small-diameter logs are limited by technical, economic, and market constraints. Small-diameter logs yield lower valued products and cost more per unit to process than do traditional large-diameter, high-quality logs. Is there a market for small-diameter logs? Is it economically feasible to produce and sell such logs? The material properties of small-diameter wood are also critical for determining suitability of use.

For instance, from the perspective of material characteristics, 6- to 13-in.-diameter ponderosa and lodgepole pine may be best suited for producing roundwood products (e.g., poles, posts, vigas, latias, house logs). Smaller (3- to 6-in.) roundwood is suitable feedstock for pulp and panel products (e.g., OSB, waferboard, particleboard). Material less than 3 in. in diameter is suitable for grape stakes, tree stakes, and orchard props. Bagged dried shavings for pet bedding is another potential product option. Residues could be used for hog fuel, wood pellets, firewood, and bark mulch.

A log sort yard should consider a mixture of commodity and specialty log products. Commodity products are standard products that serve a broad market, such as 2- by 6-in. dimension lumber, OSB panels, and engineered I-joists. Specialty products serve a smaller customer segment, taking advantage of higher niche market prices. A mixture of specialty and commodity products is often needed to diversify log sort yard opportunities to capture market share, with the major focus on standard commodity products.

Markets and Marketing

Successful log sort yard operations market products for a range of forest products businesses. Success is predicated on getting the highest net value from each log. This can be achieved by getting each log to the best available market in the most economical way. Markets must also be matched with suitable products that can be produced from the available timber resource.

The key to successful marketing is to understand the customers' needs and then satisfy these needs better than the competition can. Markets, marketing, and market feasibility are critical considerations in exploring log sort yard opportunities. Keep in mind that marketing logs is not like selling automobiles or toothpaste. Logs are sold to industrial customers, and marketing methods vary considerably from selling to the general retail market. Regardless, the focus of marketing, whether toothpaste or logs, remains the same: meeting customer needs and expectations and finding solutions to their problems (Mater and others 1992).

A market feasibility study is conducted to assess available markets for log sort yard products. Such things as target markets and market segmentation, primary and secondary processing industrial infrastructure, specialty and commodity markets, distribution, and promotion all need to be carefully analyzed and evaluated for available log markets. Market considerations also include a critical look at the industry— type of industry, competitors, wages, number of jobs, growth, and stability. Strategies developed to meet the "4-Ps" of marketing (product, place, promotion, and price) are formalized in the marketing plan. The marketing plan provides the guide for developing and distributing log sort yard products to markets (Mater and others 1992).

Sinclair (1992) poses several questions to consider in targeting markets:

- What needs and desires are currently not being satisfied by competitive products?

- How do desired benefits and choice criteria vary among potential customers?

- Which target segments, offerings, and marketing programs appeal most to customers in those segments?

- How should products from a log sort yard be positioned to differentiate them from a competitor's offerings and give the log yard firm sustainable competitive advantage?

In defining a target market, investigate the mass market and market segmentation of the log market (Sinclair 1992). Mass marketing considers all potential log buyers interested in the offerings of the sort yard. Mass marketing assumes that all customers have similar needs in relation to a particular product. For the log sort yard, this would include all wood-using businesses. Market segmentation breaks down a mass market into smaller groups of similar customers. Multiple segmentation is the combination of market segments. For example, customer segments for a log sort yard might be sawmills, veneer mills, OSB plants, and pulp mills.

Log sort yards require an established diverse primary-processing forest products industry to consume a full range of commodity, specialty, and value-added products, such as sawlogs, posts and poles, pulpwood, and boltwood. The full range of log quality, species, and diameters harvested today is generally too variable to meet the needs of any one primary wood-using plant. To be competitive, sawmills and other primary wood-using firms are specializing product and processing lines. Log requirements for specialized mills are demanding, requiring a specific log product mix. This is an opportunity for the log sort yard to capture and provide an improved log mix to various customers. Log sort yards also require markets for poor quality and low value wood and biomass from forestland restoration projects, forest fuels reduction treatments, and log sort yard debris.

The vast majority of logs processed at commercial log sort yards are used for producing commodity products such as lumber, plywood and other panel products, engineered wood, and market pulp. Given the high percentage of commodity products, a log sort yard must focus on efficient handling, low production cost, and effective marketing. Commodities are processed and distributed in bulk. For commodities, the log market sets the competitive selling price of logs.

Industry-accepted log grading rules and scaling methods establish specifications for standard log product lines. Additional specification requirements (e.g., preferred log lengths, log trim allowance) are also common. Log specifications may vary from mill to mill, but there is general agreement on basic log grades such as those established by log grading agencies.

Product differentiation for commodities is reflected in things like credit extension, timeliness of delivery, and well-manufactured logs (e.g., properly bucked with little over- or under-trim allowance). Commodity logs require moderate quality control measures to ensure conformance to product specifications (e.g., on grade, accurate log scale, proper trim allowance).

In recent years, interest has increased in purchasing small quantities of specialty logs or even individual logs from log sort yards. Interest in specialty markets for logs is likely to increase and supplements the traditional commodity log market. An example of a high-valued specialty log is bird's eye and curly maple. Naturally occurring defects in maple produce this wood, which is highly sought by furniture makers. Another high-valued specialty product is spruce tonewood for musical instruments. Even blue-stained and wormy pine is being sold to rustic furniture and door manufacturers for the Santa Fe style house market in the southwestern United States.

Another developing market for small quantities of logs provides small forest products businesses with a wood supply. A good example of this is the Ministry of Forests Vernon Log Sort and Sales Yard in British Columbia (Ministry of Forests 1999). The Vernon yard handles logs harvested under contract for the Ministry of Forests' small business timber program.

In addition, log sort yards provide specialty logs for local processors and micro-businesses, artisans, and special forest products processors. Small quantities of logs are sold to rustic furniture makers, artisans, and processors of special forest products, such as bark, conks, and burls (for turning bowls). Specialty products must be in a niche market where there is a clear demand for such products. Specialty products often return high dollar margins but at substantially lower sales volumes than do commodity products.

Semi-processed log products are becoming increasingly successful for some commercial log sort yards that incorporate satellite primary processing operations (C. Edwards, personal communication, 1999). Products include debarked logs for stud mills, fence posts and rails, landscape timbers, utility poles, and clean pulp chips. Satellite chip mills offer opportunities to merchandise higher value logs from pulpwood. Other value-added log sort yard operations include post and pole peeling mills, which produce products like utility poles, fence posts, and rails.

As the available softwood resource continues to decrease in average log diameter, some operators have captured a unique market opportunity in debarking stud logs at the log sort yard. An inventory of debarked stud logs helps the sawmill operator reduce bottlenecks at the debarker and smooth out production flow, thereby improving mill productivity (C. Edwards, personal communication, 1999). Similar reasons are given for satellite chip mills, where pulp mill raw material flow is improved and processing noise is reduced at the pulp mill.

Some operations have integrated the log sort yard with small-scale primary and secondary manufacturing such as sawmilling with flooring and furniture making. A log sort yard in Hayfork, California, has incorporated several of these types of value-added processing operations (R. Jaegel, personal communication, 1999).

Log yard debris can present a significant problem. Studies by the Forest Engineering Research Institute of Canada (FERIC) have shown that about 5% of the volume processed through a log sort yard accumulates as debris (Sinclair and Wellburn 1984). Residue markets for log sort yard debris are important because they could make the difference between profitable operations and those that struggle. Good markets and cost-efficient transportation for yard residues are essential to success. A commercial mulch operation may also be a viable alternative for yard residues, producing products such as mulch and organic fertilizer. Without a market for residues, log sort yard debris must be burned or hauled to a landfill, often at substantial expense.

Log buyers purchase logs for production in primary forest products manufacturing plants (e.g., sawmills). Large quantities of logs and other products sold at sort yards are used as raw material feedstock (e.g., sawlogs, pulpwood) and semi-processed material (e.g., peeled posts and poles, clean pulp chips, debarked stud logs). Logs are most often distributed directly to mills and other wood-using businesses.

Log brokers who purchase and distribute logs are common on the West Coast and in the southeastern United States. A limited number of log buyers serve a high geographic market concentration area. Demand can be highly cyclical, both with regard to business fluctuations and seasonal variation. Distribution channels are short where logs are bought and sold by a log broker or directly by the consuming mill. Distribution also involves the physical movement and transfer of ownership of a product from the producer to the customer (Mater and others 1992).

Transportation infrastructure is also an important consideration for the log sort yard. Moving goods to the market is a critical function of distribution, especially for bulky forest products where transportation costs can represent a significant portion of the final cost to the consumer (Sinclair 1992). Poor markets and transportation infrastructure as well as high costs limit options to move logs to market.

Trucking is the primary means of transporting logs from woods to log sort yard and log sort yard to buyer. Rail and barge transportation are reserved for large volumes of commodity products (i.e., logs and semi-processed products such as clean pulp chips). Choice of transportation mode depends on efficiency, cost, timeliness of delivery, and access to transportation. If possible, a log sort yard operator should work with their freight carrier to secure low freight rates and back hauls to reduce transportation costs. All options of transporting logs should be considered.

Good transportation and integrated infrastructure are required to realize adequate economic return to make processing a diverse log supply feasible. The lack of an industrial and transportation infrastructure is a significant barrier to effective market development and should not be overlooked or taken lightly. This situation is typical in the Southwest and Intermountain West regions of the United States. An integrated forest products industry, with the ability to utilize and market all products including log yard debris, is crucial for a log sort yard.

Direct selling by telephone calls and visits to mills is the promotion strategy of most independent log sort yards. Traditional mass-market advertising is seldom used and generally not thought to be worth the expense for such a geographically concentrated market with few players. However, on a more local scale, distribution of log specifications and price sheets is used extensively as a log sort yard advertising tool. This information may be distributed by direct mail to log buyers or used as a handout for mill visits or "cold calls." Potentially, advertising could be used effectively in regional forest products industry magazines, industry association newsletters, and local newspapers. The most recent promotional developments include the posting of promotional material and announcement of log yard sales through the Internet (RCFC 2003).

Processing

General materials handling and log processing functions, equipment, and sorting systems for log sort yards were described in a previous report (Dramm and others 2002). Preliminary log sort yard design, layout, and operations are based on principles described in that report. Raw material characteristics (e.g., log diameter distribution, total annual volume to be processed), products, and log and semi-processed markets are considered in developing an efficient log sort yard design and operation.

Consideration must be given to available log sorting technology and handling equipment and their ability to process the available resource into suitable log products. In many cases, different raw materials have different processing technology requirements. Log volume to be processed annually and piece count rate per shift dictate appropriate materials handling and processing equipment requirements for the yard. Appropriately scaled technologies and systems for a log sort yard size and application are also important for the economic feasibility analysis.

For example, while large grade logs can be efficiently sorted using a front end loader, the efficient sorting of small-diameter material may require log sorting tables or log merchandisers (Dramm and others 2002). Linear and transverse sorting machines and log merchandisers show their worth in the processing of small-diameter logs compared with conventional log sorting systems that incorporate front end or hydraulic loaders. For small-diameter logs, it may be necessary to initiate semi-processing or even primary processing at the log sort yard, such as producing clean pulp chips, debarked sawlogs, or peeled posts and poles, for the yard to be economically viable.

The solid wood volume of a log 8 in. in diameter and 10 ft long is only about 25% of that of a log 16 in. in diameter of the same length (Barbour 1999). In other words, it takes four 8-in.-diameter logs to equal the same cubic volume of wood as a 16-in.-diameter log. This means that four times as many logs must be processed to equal the same production rates achieved by processing logs with twice the average diameter.

Because log handling equipment is limited by its machine duty cycle time, log sort yard productivity is controlled more by piece count production rate than by actual volume processed. The volume of logs processed is really a function of machine lifting capacity. Consequently, processing small-diameter logs can be substantially more expensive on a per cubic volume basis than processing large-diameter logs. Increased value comes from the increased volume per log and higher quality of large-diameter logs compared with small-diameter logs.

Efficient small-diameter processing is all about substantially increasing piece count rate production, while at the same time controlling costs. What is not so apparent is the excessively high piece count rate necessary to achieve economic feasibility. That is, efficient, cost-effective, high piece count rate production is critical in processing small logs. This is achieved with the use of specialized materials handling, processing, and sorting equipment. The purchase price for specialized materials handling equipment such as log stackers and crawler track mounted hydraulic log loaders easily exceeds $500,000. The construction of log merchandisers and other log factories can cost several million dollars. Consequently, a much higher log volume production is required to spread out and recover capitalization costs. For this reason, processing small-diameter logs requires a substantially larger scale log sort yard operation in comparison with that required by processing higher value large logs.

Sinclair and Wellburn (1984) point out the competitive advantages of small-, medium-, and large-scale log sort yards. In large yards, fixed costs are spread out over a greater volume of logs, effectively reducing per unit costs. Consequently, medium-sized log sort yards are somewhat at a disadvantage because they are not able to use the economies of scale used by large yards. Medium-sized yards also require fairly heavy capital investment in construction and equipment, unlike small yards, which can be developed with minimal construction costs. Where limited log supply rules out a large-scale sort yard operation, a medium-sized yard may be feasible for sorting small-diameter logs and have a competitive advantage over a small-scale yard.

Log prices paid to the log sort yard operator are directly related to the value of logs sold to mills, which is based on product volume recovery and wood quality yield. The value of products from small-diameter material can be substantially lower than that for large logs (Fig. 3). For example, products from large-diameter ponderosa pine may average $800 to $900/thousand board feet (lumber tally) and products from small-diameter logs may yield only $200/thousand board feet (lumber tally).

Given the reduced value per cubic foot and at one-fourth the volume, an 8-in.-diameter log may be valued at less than 10% the value of a 16-in.-diameter log of the same species and length. Yet, on a per piece basis, it may cost only slightly more to process a large log than a small log. As a consequence, opportunities to process small-diameter logs can be very limited. This is especially true if there is not a sufficient mix of larger high value logs and sufficiently large average diameter of logs processed in the log sort yard (Majestic Forest Management 1997).

On a related issue, material flow and balance are critical to log sort yard layout and design. Unfortunately, these are often not given sufficient consideration. Projected volume to be processed in the proposed sort yard should be converted to number of pieces so that efficient log sort yard design and performance requirements for materials handling equipment can be specified. Note again that as log diameter decreases, piece count increases dramatically for the same board footage log scale. This relationship increases exponentially as log diameter decreases.

For example, a log sort yard with an annual production of 11 million ft^3 that processes an average size log of 9-in. diameter, 16-ft long, will process about 1.25 million logs annually or 5,000 logs/day. A similar yard that processes the same cubic volume annually but with an average SED of 18 in. (and 16 ft length) will process less than 1,400 logs/day, or about one-fourth as many logs. To roughly estimate piece count processing capability requirements, divide the total log volume by the log scale volume per log for a typical log (i.e., average diameter, taper, and length). Note that a more detailed analysis can be done by breaking down logs by length and diameter distribution classes for a more accurate estimate of piece count.

Material handling is another important consideration. There is a cost for each time a log is picked up, transported, and set down (Mason 1998). For illustrative purposes, let's say that the handling cost is $5. The challenge is, How many times can you afford to handle a $100 log? How many times can you afford to handle a $4 log if it costs $5 to handle it? Processing a $4 log does not make any sense if it costs $5 each time you handle it.

One solution for cost-effective processing of $4 logs is to accumulate, handle, and process the logs in bunches rather than individually. Another option is to reduce the handling cost by making those processes requiring individual log handling very efficient. For example, the use of a high production log sorting systems and log merchandisers are more efficient, hence economical, for processing small logs in comparison with sorting logs with a front end loader. Other examples include the adoption of weight scaling instead of stick scaling and transporting bunched logs using the full capacity of transport machines. (Refer to the discussion on

lowering the cost curve for marginal logs in the section on economics (Fig. 4).)

Recent developments in log sort yard operations are making the processing of small-diameter, low-value logs more economical. The most notable has been the adoption of log merchandising systems, which were developed in the 1970s for softwood sawmills to optimize log grade and value recovery in bucking long logs into short log products (Dramm and others 2002). Under the right market pricing conditions, log merchandising can capture higher valued sawlogs from pulpwood logs. Log merchandising systems may be associated with satellite chip mills and process very large volumes of small-diameter logs. The development of smaller scale systems has been under investigation by several groups, and these systems are now commercially available.

Finally, in considering log sort yard equipment and design, choosing the proper handling and processing equipment is critical. It is not good practice to use machines where full capacity cannot be utilized most of the time (i.e., equipment that is over-designed for the job). Over-designing the log sort yard or equipment can dramatically increase investment and operating costs. Less expensive machines with inadequate capacity or even the wrong piece of equipment is frequently purchased to reduce investment costs, only to be lost elsewhere. Over- or under-designing handling equipment or choosing the wrong type of equipment limits log sort yard viability.

Several log sort yard designs should be considered initially to compare their economic feasibility. At this point of the process, it is important to identify the technical feasibility of sorting and handling logs efficiently. This is accomplished by considering the principles described by Dramm and others (2002), Sinclair and Wellburn (1984), and Hampton (1981), along with the principles outlined in the previous discussion. The log processing system must match the volume and size (log diameter) distribution for the number of projected log sorts. The log sort yard must be balanced with the appropriate piece production rate and volume anticipated. A logical general log sort yard design is often found, and the basic economic question then becomes, How many log sorts should there be given the raw material and available markets?

Financial Analysis

Financial analysis of the potential log sort yard investment is performed to assess economic viability. This section provides a general overview of financial analysis and is intended for the log sort yard project planning team, who provide information to a business finance specialist for developing the necessary financial *pro forma* projections. This section does not include a detailed description of intermediate financial feasibility analysis and development of log sort yard *pro forma*. These subjects warrant a separate technical report.

Most log sort yards operate either as an independent business or as part of a larger integrated company. This includes community yards that may be set up as cooperative or corporately owned by the community. Consequently, this section focuses on standard business financial analysis. Note that government yards handle log sort yard financial analysis somewhat differently. However, because a private log sort yard contractor is generally retained to operate government yards, the following discussion will be of interest to those operations as well.

The financial analysis develops *pro forma* projections for the log sort yard operation and provides the basis for financial justification for business startup or expansion. These projections are used to determine the likelihood of financial success. Financial analysis takes into account a number of business financing principles and concepts, including depreciation, taxes, methods of discounting cash flows, and calculation of after-tax net cash flow and net present value. Combined with market feasibility, the financial analysis provides the basis of a business plan for the log sort yard.

Pro forma also provides the best overall basis for monitoring business performance after the enterprise is established. *Pro forma* financials include the following:

- Projections of income

- Projections of value of assets, liabilities, and net worth

- Working capital requirements

- Calculation of cash flow

- Projections of cash, shipments, receivables, payables, and other operational statistics

- Sensitivity analysis

To be a viable business venture, the log sort yard must be justifiable as a stand-alone profitable operation or as an incremental investment associated with an existing business, where the operation of the yard produces a stream of cost savings for the existing business that would justify the investment. Benefits need to be documented and quantified with regard to potential for increased profitability, cost control, or risk reduction. Benefits could include improved sorting and scaling, higher value from log merchandising, reduced transportation costs, better inventory control, or other reductions in operating costs (Sinclair and Wellburn 1984).

Note that it might be possible to justify a log sort yard on the basis of achieving intangible social or environmental benefits. There is no published literature in support of this new concept. The limited Canadian experience (see Community and Government Yards) is inconclusive. Log sort yards in the United States have had difficulties along these lines, but the reasons for failure or success are not well documented and deserve further study.

Proposed log sort yard projects should be evaluated on an after-tax net cash flow (ATNCF) basis to reflect a real cash flow and income statement (Govett 2001). The net present value (NPV) is the best way to measure financial performance, rather than payback and internal rate of return (IRR).

Appropriate working capital is critically important. If there is a single, greatest problem with most business planning, it is lack of appropriate focus on working capital requirements. Only rarely are working capital requirements adequately considered by those who lack business and business planning experience and in many cases are not even considered. Working capital is frequently underestimated.

Attention to cash flow is a critical aspect of *pro forma* financial feasibility, as it is precisely this part of the analysis that helps to best define the prospective working capital needs. Lack of attention to cash flow and its associated impact on working capital requirements can easily result in the failure of a business that has the potential for profitable operation. Cash flow projections carefully look at the timing of cash inflow compared with that of cash outflow, such that solid estimates of working capital requirements can be considered and planned. Inadequate attention to cash flow can easily result in a circumstance where a log sort yard lacks the ability to meet its financial obligations, because the cash to meet those obligations is not yet in hand.

Attention to cash flow is important for all businesses and is particularly important for small businesses, especially those with seasonal aspects. Give special attention to cash flow analysis where (1) a business may have to maintain a generally large inventory that increases and decreases with the season, (2) suppliers are dependant on prompt payment for raw material provided, and (3) customers may be expected to pay slowly on a routine or occasional basis.

Lenders are typically only peripherally interested in measures of overall financial performance, but they are very interested in the demonstration of the ability to make payments on borrowed principal and interest. Cash flow projections are of greatest interest to lenders, and they are very important to the log sort yard operator as well. These projections should be an integral part of the analysis. Lenders want to see your ability to pay back principal and interest. A very simple way to provide cash flow projections is as a series of line items following the series of calculations, including after-tax profit and after-tax net cash flow projections, in which the first line shows the period for the initial loan principal, the second line shows the principal repayment, and the final line shows the outstanding loan balance at the end of each period.

With few exceptions, leasing of materials handling and production equipment is usually not advisable because leased equipment cannot be depreciated. Depreciation needs to be considered as an integral part of the analysis. Look beyond after-tax profit and focus on after-tax net cash flow. Sole consideration of after-tax profit gives a distorted picture in which many potentially viable projects are killed and in which leasing will usually appear favorable. The best approach is to conduct the analysis using both leasing and purchase options, and then consider the best course of action. In focusing on after-tax profit, leasing options will typically appear attractive. This is because the lease payment may be similar to the combined interest payment on loan and depreciation associated with the purchase option. The after-tax profit is typically similar under the two options, but the overall investment is lower under the lease option, hence making the lease appear more attractive. However, depreciation is an expense that the business pays to itself, and as such is combined with after-tax profit in determining after-tax net cash flow. Focusing on this measure under the two options can help to provide a better understanding of the pros and cons of leasing and purchasing.

The need to fully and completely justify all assumptions cannot be overemphasized. Furthermore, it is important to understand which assumptions are critical to the analysis. Several variables are needed for a log sort yard financial analysis to generate *pro forma* financial statements. These include assumptions about production, payroll, manufacturing costs, capital investments, estimation of depreciation, cash flow, market and financial assumptions, product prices, and development, raw material, operating, and administrative log sort yard costs. Again, always ask "Why this value?" for each assumption and document your reasons for choosing the values for each variable. Expect that you will need to explain and justify each assumption to the lender or key decision-maker.

Management

Careful consideration must be given to how the log sort yard will be structured and managed. This includes an assessment of the management team (e.g., log yard contractor) who will manage and operate the yard:

- Do key management personnel have the experience and know-how to run a log sort yard?

- What business controls will be used to ensure a viable venture?

- Who are the business advisors, i.e., the board of directors, to help guide the venture? (lender, attorney, accountant, marketer, and manufacturing and procurement experts)

Business management resources and information are readily available and are not covered in this paper. In addition, financial and business technical assistance for business startup and expansion is readily available from agencies such as the Small Business Administration (SBA) and Small Business Development Centers (SBDCs). Both provide a number of resources on business management, finance, and marketing issues. Business consultants and accountants also provide a wide range of services of interest.

Safety, Health, and Environmental Issues

Non-financial factors, including safety and environmental concerns, take priority over financial measures. Safety, health, and environmental issues could become a limiting consideration in an otherwise successful venture. For example, concerns could arise regarding waste wood residues, log yard surface water runoff, operation of mobile equipment in close proximity of yard workers, and safety and health standards and codes. It is necessary to overcome any environmental or safety problems that might occur. The economic cost of meeting such regulations must be factored into the financial *pro forma* analysis. Regulations and permits are important considerations and must be in place before construction of the yard can begin. Although the Federal government sets minimum regulatory standards, States are generally responsible for enforcement. Standards can be highly variable from State to State. Refer to your State government for more information.

Next Steps

Economics and feasibility are just the first steps in establishing and operating a log sort yard. The next steps involve layout, design, construction, and eventual operation. Dramm and others (2002) gives a general review of concepts important in evaluating these next steps. Sinclair and Wellburn (1984) and Hampton (1981) provide extensive discussions on these subjects, especially for large-scale log sort yards. The following is a brief description of layout and design, construction, and management of log sort yards.

Layout and Design

An initial study of log sort yard alternative layouts and designs will save money in the long run. Layout and design are jointly considered to find an optimal log sort yard configuration. Yard layout considerations influence yard design, while design elements influence yard layout. The best yard layout depends on the size of logs to be handled, volume of logs to be processed, site restrictions, and capital available for material handling systems (Sinclair and Wellburn 1984). Selection of an optimal layout and design is determined by evaluating the cost alternatives—What is most economically feasible? Yard layout should logically fit with the flow of log handling operations, considering all log sort yard functions, which include unloading and reloading, log roll-out areas for grading and scaling, scaling method, log merchandising, sorting system, and log storage. Other considerations include fire protection and safety, log yard

Figure 6—Automated log merchandiser system for merchandising and sorting sawlogs from pulpwood material. (Photo by Rusty Dramm, USDA Forest Service)

debris management, and compliance with environmental regulations.

Industrial engineering concepts can be employed to aid in the layout and design of log sort yards for efficient and economical operation (Sinclair 1984). Industrial engineering concepts help improve log flow through the yard, reduce bottlenecks, and minimize the need for subsequent changes to the yard. Operations management stresses a systematic approach to problem solving and finding an optimal layout and design (Baldwin 1984). Industrial engineering methods used in layout and design include materials handling theory, productivity analysis, quality control, log storage and inventory control, queuing (waiting lines) theory, and analysis of process flow (flow chart).

Two basic manufacturing production systems are used by log sort yards: production line and batch processing. In a production line, logs move directly from one operation to the next by mechanical transport systems (e.g., transfer chains and tables). This system has gained in popularity in log sort yard design, especially for processing low-value and small-diameter logs. An example is the use of a log merchandiser system to sort sawlogs from pulpwood material (Fig. 6). Batch processing is by either position or processing layouts. In a position layout, the location of each batch of logs is fixed and the mobile log sorting machines move to each batch for processing. Less common is the process-oriented layout, where logs are transported from one area to the next by mobile equipment in a series of separate, fixed log

grading and scaling, merchandising, and sorting equipment stations.

Medium to large yards may incorporate one or more of these production systems. Small yards are usually restricted to a position layout for batch processing of logs. Advances in log sorting systems and log merchandisers may make it economical to employ production line systems in small-scale yards. Such systems may even be necessary for the economic sorting of small logs regardless of yard size (Roger Jaegel, personal communication, 1999).

Yard Construction

Civil engineering aspects of yard construction involve yard siting analysis, site survey, soil sampling, surface drainage survey, location of access roads, sources of construction materials, and sites for disposal of waste construction materials and yard debris (Sinclair and Wellburn 1984). These aspects are used to develop a detailed engineering plan for the yard. A surveying or civil engineering firm should be retained to perform these jobs.

The log sort yard project manager/engineer develops a construction program from the engineering plan. The program typically includes construction schedule, contracts, and purchasing, inspection, and cost control measures. Before construction can begin, the proper State and local permits and licenses must be secured. This is the responsibility of the project manager (Mater Engineering 1998).

Log sort yard construction can be a major project for large yards. A general contractor is selected to manage the actual construction of the yard. It is the general contractor's responsibility to maintain the construction schedule, hire subcontractors, and arrange for the construction materials and supplies. Options include hiring a construction contractor or consulting engineer as the general contractor to manage the construction of the yard. A company with enough experience in log sort yard type projects may choose to be its own general contractor. Small log sort yards may require minimal construction, especially if former mill sites or other comparable industrial sites can be found.

A major portion of construction is the clearing, stripping, grading, and surfacing of the yard proper. Earth moving equipment depends on the size of the yard and site conditions. Material for surfacing the yard depends on the size of the yard operation, machine duty cycle, and machine travel speeds. Buildings and structures typically include an office, maintenance and supply shed, truck scales (if weight scaling), refueling station, and drainage structures (culverts, drainage ditches). Other improvements to the property include utility service hookups like water, sewer (if within a municipality), electrical, and telephone.

Management and Operation

Most log sort yards should operate as a business. For tax purposes, several business forms are available, including corporation, partnership, limited liability corporation (LLC), sole proprietor, and cooperative. Log yards operating within an integrated firm are dictated by the business form of the firm. The exceptions to this are log sort yards not subject to taxation, such as government-operated yards. Community log sort yards are generally organized as cooperatives or corporations owned by the community (e.g., RCFC).

Yard operations begin with the selection and training of supervisors and yard crew and decisions regarding the organizational structure, accounting and scaling systems, cost control, and marketing and operating plans. Efficient operation of the yard requires a balance between product quality and operational productivity. In addition to physical operations, crucial management concerns include receiving, shipping, inventory accounting, and accurate log scaling.

As in any manufacturing setting, day-to-day log sort yard operations are routine—logs are unloaded, graded, scaled, sorted, and reloaded (Dramm and others 2002). After startup challenges and day-to-day operations have been smoothed out, effort should focus on assessing log sort yard performance and making quality and productivity improvements. This covers all phases of the operation, from procurement to balancing yard productivity and quality, marketing and sales, safety, and employee training.

Conclusions and Recommendations

This publication discusses basic marketing and economic concepts, planning approach, and feasibility methodology for assessing log sort yard operations. A log sort yard must be justifiable by measures of its ability to meet stated objectives, whether for profit, cost savings, risk reduction, or intangible social and environmental benefits. This last objective is the subject of the authors' investigation into the applications of log sort yards. Special attention is given to sorting small-diameter and underutilized logs from forest restoration, fuels reduction, and thinning operations. Development of log sort yards may provide opportunities to improve the utilization of small-diameter and underutilized material from such forestry operations.

Although commercial log sort yards have a proven track record throughout North America, small community-based and government-operated log yards have had limited success. Operating a log sort yard requires experience in several disciplines, such as log procurement, log markets, manufacturing systems, industrial safety, and business management. Serious consideration must be given to employing an experienced log sort yard contractor to operate and manage day-to-day operations. Commercial, community, and government log sort yards operate successfully under business management organization and principles.

Several operational, policy, and judicial issues need to be resolved for government and community log sort yards to operate successfully in the United States. For example, guarantee of a consistent timber supply is the long-term major overriding issue to establish and maintain a viable forest products business, including a log sort yard. Until the issues surrounding the delivery of a continuous supply of material are resolved, small-diameter log sort yards are not likely to succeed.

Economics

Small-diameter logs yield substantially lower product value and cost more per unit to process than do traditional large-diameter, high-quality logs. As log diameter decreases, piece count increases dramatically for the same log volume. Log sort yard equipment productivity is most limited by the piece count production rate. The smaller the average diameter processed, the increasingly expensive the log becomes to handle and process.

Sorting small-diameter logs presents several challenges that require efficient log handling at minimum unit cost. Small softwood logs offer moderate and relatively uniform quality and low volume per piece, which require high production with minimal handling to be economical. The characteristic uniformity and moderate quality of small-diameter logs also make it difficult to recover enough value-added to justify effort to grade, scale, and sort these logs. The economic dilemma of the log cost/value relationship is not good news for those interested in small-diameter log sort yards. Higher value logs in the log procurement mix are crucial for log-sort yard viability (Majestic Forest Management 1997).

Marginal logs are characterized by low-value, small-diameter, and underutilized materials. To be economically viable, a log sort yard must process logs better than the average marginal log. As log diameter decreases, log value decreases and log costs escalate. The line of marginality defines the log diameter where log cost equals log value—the diameter breakpoint between profit and loss. Logs with diameters smaller than the marginal log diameter are more expensive than their inherent value.

Canadian government and community log sort yards could serve as models for similar operations in the United States. The Canadian strategy is to improve log product mix procured and reduce the number of marginal logs processed through the yard. Their experience shows that a primary key to financial success is the ability to sell a high percentage of high-value premium logs and not process small-diameter logs through the yard. Nevertheless, a recent downturn in Canadian wood product markets resulted in poor financial performance of these log sort yards. This research finding has serious negative implications for log sort yard utilization and marketing of low-valued, small-diameter material.

Another option to consider is subsidizing the excessive costs of small-diameter materials. As small-diameter material frequently costs substantially more than the value of potential products that could be produced from this resource, a subsidy might be necessary to defray excessive costs. Subsidizing small-diameter material may be a small price to pay, considering the alternative of expensive forest restoration, forest fuels treatments, and risk of catastrophic wildfire and consequent risk to natural resources, property, and life.

The solution to the small-diameter problem (i.e., marginal logs) is to lower costs or increase value of logs to be able to use small-diameter material economically. This is difficult to achieve and any hopes to do so lie with taking an objective planning approach to find viable opportunities to plan and operate a successful small-diameter log sort yard.

Planned Programming Approach

Log sort yard projects are too often based on subjective opinions rather than objective investigation. This can quickly turn into a deep emotional attachment for the project as extensive effort, time, energy, and money are expended, despite little hope for success. The authors recommend a planned programming approach to log sort yard development. This approach ultimately leads to strategic, marketing, business, and operational plans to help guide the development and operation of the log sort yard.

Beyond initial planning and feasibility, the next steps in developing a log sort yard involve layout and design, construction, and operation. Small log sort yards may require minimal construction, especially if former mill sites or other comparable industrial sites can be found.

Feasibility

Determination of preliminary feasibility should begin early in the planning process as it helps focus efforts on potentially viable opportunities and saves time, effort, and money from being spent on chasing poor investment scenarios. Of most importance to log sort yard planners in conducting preliminary feasibility is the evaluation of gross margins. Positive gross margins indicate scenarios worth further investigation and more intensive financial analysis. Negative gross margins indicate nonviable scenarios not worth further investigation. Any options that do not look promising (those with negative gross margins) under the preliminary best-case scenarios should be dropped. Others, even the marginal options, can be explored further. After options have been narrowed, detailed resource assessment, markets, and financial analyses are done.

Several critical factors are considered and evaluated for each log sort yard scenario under consideration. Each log sorting option should be evaluated in relation to each factor. These include raw material (timber) resource, product options, market feasibility, materials handling and processing technology, financial analysis, management expertise, and safety, health, and environmental considerations. Assumptions about raw material resource, products, markets, costs, prices, and other factors used in feasibility analysis are critically important. The need to be able to fully and completely justify all assumptions cannot be underscored enough. Furthermore, it is important to understand which assumptions are critical to the analysis.

Recommendations

Every consideration should be driven by the need to procure logs and process them at the lowest unit cost possible and to minimize inventory and overhead costs. At the same time, it is essential to recover the highest value from the logs processed in the yard. Log merchandising and sorting for highest net value and negotiating the highest possible product prices in the log market result in the highest log value.

Optimization of log processing is key to recovering the greatest overall potential net value for log products. Optimizing value is achieved by

- log merchandising (i.e., bucking and sorting tree length-long logs into various log products such as peeler blocks, sawlogs and pulpwood),

- cutting back sawlog length to veneer specifications on those logs that can be upgraded to veneer logs and peeler blocks,

- semi-processing (e.g., peeling posts and poles, debarking stud bolts/logs, and chipping pulp logs), and

- controlling losses from insect, decay, and stain.

Log quality control (QC) is also critical in capturing the greatest potential log value. This involves tightening sloppy log making practices, reducing the number of misbucked logs, and ensuring that logs are manufactured to proper lengths and log damage is minimized. Procedures range from simple QC checklist evaluation of log making quality to more involved statistical process control (SPC) methods.

In terms of marketing, when effort has been expended to improve the best product mix for highest potential product value, it makes no sense to sell logs at less than premium prices. An aggressive marketing effort is the best and least costly way to improve the overall value of the log products produced. Good marketing is the best way to improve productivity, followed closely by log product optimization and quality control efforts.

Production rate is also important, especially in minimizing per unit costs. However, this should not be at the expense of product quality whereby pushing production rates results in loss of product value because of out-of-specification products. Log sort yard production rate and control of processing and product quality must be balanced. Effort to ensure quality is more important for higher value products where downfall would result in substantial value loss. In fact, as the quality of the log making process is improved, production rates may improve as process flow and processing are improved. The general procedure is to bring the log sort yard up to acceptable production rates, then work to control product quality and improve processing efficiency.

The key to minimizing costs and recovering the highest value is log sort yard efficiency. The most important factor in reducing log handling costs is to reduce the number of moves, the so-called "picks" (i.e., pickup, transport, and set down) in the log sort yard (Mason 1998). This requires careful consideration of log sort yard layout and design based on the log characteristics and number of sorts.

Procurement and Marketing Focus

Focus log sort yard startup on log procurement and marketing of the available resource to available markets. To begin, stay focused on securing and moving logs to current markets (such as in log brokering where you do not actually take ownership). Then, look at other opportunities for log sorting, and, finally, perhaps explore semi-processing and value-added manufacturing.

Log procurement and marketing do not require much capital expenditure. If successful, other opportunities to expand the business can be explored. If not successful, you have effectively protected yourself by limiting potential financial losses (such as collateral used to secure financing the business). When markets are established and log supply is secured, the next logical step is construction of the log sort yard. Eventually, it may be feasible to add semi-processing and value-added operations.

Taking this approach will help place focus on the two most important issues facing all forest products ventures: resource procurement and marketing. Again, guarantee of a consistent timber supply is a long-term major overriding issue for establishing and maintaining a viable forest products business, including a log sort yard operation (Mater Engineering 1998). Similarly, marketing and market feasibility are very important considerations when exploring log sort yard opportunities. Both issues are major challenges to solve but can be done with limited risk.

Sources of Information

Several sources of related information and technical assistance are available. Contacts for technical assistance for log sort yard planning, planning information for forest products businesses, and statistical business data are provided in Appendix B. Appendix C provides published information useful for the log sort yard planner.

Literature Cited

Alden, H.A. 1995. Hardwoods of North America. Gen. Tech. Rep. FPL–GTR–83. Madison, WI: U.S. Department of Agriculture, Forest Service, Forest Products Laboratory. 136 p.

Alden, H.A. 1997. Softwoods of North America. Gen. Tech. Rep. FPL–GTR–102. , Madison, WI: U.S. Department of Agriculture, Forest Service, Forest Products Laboratory. 1,516 p.

Baldwin, R.F. 1984. Operations management in the forest products industry. San Francisco, CA. Miller Freeman Publications. 264 p.

Bangs, D.H. Jr. 1995. The business planning guide: creating a plan for success in your own business. . Chicago, IL: Upstart Publishing Company, Inc., a Division of Dearborn Publishing Group, Inc. 208 p.

Barbour, J.R. 1999. Relationship between diameter and gross product value for small trees. In: Proceedings, Wood Technology Clinic and Show Conference, Portland, OR. San Francisco, CA: Miller Freeman Publications.

Bryan, E.L. 1996. The best possible sawmill: a guidebook for the high-tech journey ahead. San Francisco, CA: Miller Freeman Publications. 231 p.

Dramm, J.R. 1999. Small-diameter issues and opportunities. In: Proceedings from Wood Technology Clinic and Show Conference, Portland, OR. San Francisco, CA: Miller Freeman Publications.

Dramm, J.R.; Jackson, G. 2000. Is it time to revisit the log sort yard? Proceedings from Wood Technology Clinic and Show Conference, Portland, OR. Miller Freeman Publications, San Francisco, CA.

Dramm, J.R.; Jackson, G.L.; Wong, J. 2002. Review of log sort yards. FPL–GTR–132. Madison, WI: U.S. Department of Agriculture, Forest Service, Forest Products Laboratory. 39 p.

Entrepreneur Magazine. 1995. Small business advisor. New York, NY: John Wiley & Sons, Inc. 664 p.

Forest Products Laboratory. 1999. Wood handbook—Wood as an engineering material. Gen. Tech. Rep. FPL–GTR–113. Madison, WI: U.S. Department of Agriculture, Forest Service, Forest Products Laboratory. 463 p.

Govett, R. 2001. Forest products business spreadsheets. Workshop materials. Stevens Point, WI: University of Wisconsin–Stevens Point.

Hallock, H. 1964. Some thoughts on marginal sawlogs. Forest Products Journal. 14(11): 535–539.

Hampton, C.M. 1981. Dry land log handling and sorting: planning, constructing, and operation of log yards. San Francisco, CA: Miller Freeman Publications, Inc. 215 p.

Howe, J.; Bratkovich, S. 1995. A planning guide for small and medium size wood products companies: the keys to success. NA–TP–09–95. U.S. St. Paul, MN: Department of Agriculture, Forest Service, Northeastern Area, State & Private Forestry.

Majestic Forest Management. 1997. Feasibility analysis of log yards in the Mortice TSA and Lakes TSA. Vancouver, BC: Lakes Development Society. Majestic Forest Management.

Mason, H.C. 1998. Small log processing. In: Proceedings, Wood Technology Clinic and Show Conference, Portland, OR. San Francisco, CA: Miller Freeman Publications.

Mater Engineering. 1998. Feasibility analysis for development of an incubator/log sort and sales yard facility at Hayfork. Corvallis, OR: Hayfork Watershed Research and Training Center. Mater Engineering,

Mater, J. 1988. Forest products marketing and industrial strategy operations guide. Corvallis, OR: Mater Engineering, 254 p.

Mater, J.M.; Mater, S.; Mater, C.M. 1992. Marketing forest products. . San Francisco, CA: Miller Freeman, Inc. 290 p.

Ministry of Forests. 1999. Vernon log yard review: an internal Ministry of Forests review of the Vernon log yard operations 1996/97–1998/99. Victoria, BC: Forest Enterprise Branch, Ministry of Forests.

RCFC. 2003. Revelstoke, BC, Canada: Revelstoke Community Forest Corporation.

Sinclair, S.A. 1992. Forest products marketing. New York, NY: McGraw–Hill, Inc. 403 p.

Sinclair, A.W.J.; Wellburn, G.V. 1984. A handbook for designing, building, and operating a log sort yard. Vancouver, BC. Canada: Forest Engineering Research Institute of Canada. 285 p.

State of Wisconsin. 1989. A pulp mill siting feasibility study for Wisconsin. Madison, WI: Commissioned by Governor Tommy Thompson. State of Wisconsin. 416 p.

Wallowa Resources. 1997. The potential of log sort yards: lessons from Libby, Montana and British Columbia. Wallowa Res. Rep. 2. Enterprise, OR: Wallowa Resources.

Williston, E.M. 1988. Lumber manufacturing: the design and operation of sawmills and planer mills, revised. San Francisco, CA: Miller Freeman Publications, Inc. 486 p.

Appendix A—Preliminary Feasibility Analysis

e>> Analysis Label >>>>>>>

LOG-SORT YARD PRELIMINARY FEASIBILITY ANALYSIS

MIXED SOFTWOOD LOGS - EXAMPLE RUN

Developed by: Dr. Robert Govett, University Of Wisconsin - Stevens Point and
John "Rusty" Dramm, Technology Marketing Unit, Madison, Wisconsin
Phone: 608-231-9326 or E-mail: jdramm@fs.fed.us

Beta Test Version 05.03.03

DEFINITION OF LOG INPUT VARIABLES

	Log Species /Grade (delivered to yard)	Log Price ($/unit log scale, delivered to yard)	Log Sorting Cost ($/unit delivered log scale basis)	Board Foot Log Scale (study test logs)
e>> Log Species/Grade "A"	Ponderosa P	$300.00	$60.00	720
e>> Log Species/Grade "B"	Douglas-fir	$320.00	$65.00	2,760
e>> Log Species/Grade "C"	Pulpwood	$75.00	$95.00	1,980
e>> Log Species/Grade "D"	Woods Run	$180.00	$75.00	5,240
e>> Log Species/Grade "E"	(spare)	$0.00	$0.00	0

DEFINITION OF LOG OUTPUT VARIABLES

	Log Use Sort Category (Output)	Log Mkt. Price (Output) $/unit	Log Scale Unit Volume After Sorting in Log Use Sort Category By Log Species/Grade					Value of Logs After Sorting in Log Use Sort Category By Log Species/Grade (Input)				
			Ponderosa P	Douglas-fir	Pulpwood	Woods Run	(spare)	Ponderosa P	Douglas-fir	Pulpwood	Woods Run	(spare)
e>> Log Use/Sort "A"	Veneer Peeler	$950.00	0	160	0	0	0	$0.00	$152.00	$0.00	$0.00	$0.00
e>> Log Use/Sort "B"	Pine Sawlog	$650.00	130	0	0	80	0	$84.50	$0.00	$0.00	$52.00	$0.00
e>> Log Use/Sort "C"	D-F Sawlog	$600.00	0	290	0	410	0	$0.00	$174.00	$0.00	$246.00	$0.00
e>> Log Use/Sort "D"	D-F Saw Bolt	$500.00	0	1,985	480	2,090	0	$0.00	$992.50	$240.00	$1,045.00	$0.00
e>> Log Use/Sort "E"	Poles	$400.00	520	0	0	0	0	$208.00	$0.00	$0.00	$0.00	$0.00
e>> Log Use/Sort "F"	Fiberwood	$60.00	0	105	0	260	0	$0.00	$6.30	$0.00	$15.60	$0.00
e>> Log Use/Sort "G"	Pulpwood	$60.00	0	140	1,480	2,340	0	$0.00	$8.40	$88.80	$140.40	$0.00
e>> Log Use/Sort "H"	Firewood	$5.00	70	80	20	60	0	$0.35	$0.40	$0.10	$0.30	$0.00
e>> Log Use/Sort "I"	(spare)	$0.00	0	0	0	0	0	$0.00	$0.00	$0.00	$0.00	$0.00
e>> Log Use/Sort "J"	(spare)	$0.00	0	0	0	0	0	$0.00	$0.00	$0.00	$0.00	$0.00
e>> Log Use/Sort "K"	(spare)	$0.00	0	0	0	0	0	$0.00	$0.00	$0.00	$0.00	$0.00
e>> Log Use/Sort "L"	(spare)	$0.00	0	0	0	0	0	$0.00	$0.00	$0.00	$0.00	$0.00
e>> Log Use/Sort "M"	(spare)	$0.00	0	0	0	0	0	$0.00	$0.00	$0.00	$0.00	$0.00
e>> Log Use/Sort "N"	(spare)	$0.00	0	0	0	0	0	$0.00	$0.00	$0.00	$0.00	$0.00
e>> Log Use/Sort "O"	(spare)	$0.00	0	0	0	0	0	$0.00	$0.00	$0.00	$0.00	$0.00
e>> Log Use/Sort "P"	(spare)	$0.00	0	0	0	0	0	$0.00	$0.00	$0.00	$0.00	$0.00
e>> Log Use/Sort "Q"	(spare)	$0.00	0	0	0	0	0	$0.00	$0.00	$0.00	$0.00	$0.00
e>> Log Use/Sort "R"	(spare)	$0.00	0	0	0	0	0	$0.00	$0.00	$0.00	$0.00	$0.00
e>> Log Use/Sort "S"	(spare)	$0.00	0	0	0	0	0	$0.00	$0.00	$0.00	$0.00	$0.00
e>> Log Use/Sort "T"	(spare)	$0.00	0	0	0	0	0	$0.00	$0.00	$0.00	$0.00	$0.00
e>> Log Use/Sort "U"	(spare)	$0.00	0	0	0	0	0	$0.00	$0.00	$0.00	$0.00	$0.00
e>> Log Use/Sort "V"	(spare)	$0.00	0	0	0	0	0	$0.00	$0.00	$0.00	$0.00	$0.00
e>> Log Use/Sort "W"	(spare)	$0.00	0	0	0	0	0	$0.00	$0.00	$0.00	$0.00	$0.00
e>> Log Use/Sort "X"	(spare)	$0.00	0	0	0	0	0	$0.00	$0.00	$0.00	$0.00	$0.00
e>> Log Use/Sort "Y"	(spare)	$0.00	0	0	0	0	0	$0.00	$0.00	$0.00	$0.00	$0.00
e>> Log Use/Sort "Z"	(spare)	$0.00	0	0	0	0	0	$0.00	$0.00	$0.00	$0.00	$0.00
	TOTAL >>		720	2,760	1,980	5,240	0	$292.85	$1,333.60	$328.90	$1,499.30	$0.00

Percent Volume After Sorting in Log Use Sort Category — By Log Species/Grade / Percent Value After Sorting of Log Use Sort Category — By Log Species/Grade

Log Use Sort (Output)		Log Mkt. Price (Output) $/unit	Volume Ponderosa P	Volume Douglas-fir	Volume Pulpwood	Volume Woods Run	Volume (spare)	Value Ponderosa P	Value Douglas-fir	Value Pulpwood	Value Woods Run	Value (spare)
Log Use/Sort "A"	Veneer Peeler	$950.00	0.00%	5.80%	0.00%	0.00%	0.00%	0.00%	11.40%	0.00%	0.00%	0.00%
Log Use/Sort "B"	Pine Sawlog	$650.00	18.06%	0.00%	0.00%	1.53%	0.00%	28.85%	0.00%	0.00%	3.47%	0.00%
Log Use/Sort "C"	D-F Sawlog	$600.00	0.00%	10.51%	0.00%	7.82%	0.00%	0.00%	13.05%	0.00%	16.41%	0.00%
Log Use/Sort "D"	D-F Saw Bolt	$500.00	0.00%	71.92%	24.24%	39.89%	0.00%	0.00%	74.42%	72.97%	69.70%	0.00%
Log Use/Sort "E"	Poles	$400.00	72.22%	0.00%	0.00%	0.00%	0.00%	71.03%	0.00%	0.00%	0.00%	0.00%
Log Use/Sort "F"	Fiberwood	$60.00	0.00%	3.80%	0.00%	4.96%	0.00%	0.00%	0.47%	0.00%	1.04%	0.00%
Log Use/Sort "G"	Pulpwood	$60.00	0.00%	5.07%	74.75%	44.66%	0.00%	0.00%	0.63%	27.00%	9.36%	0.00%
Log Use/Sort "H"	Firewood	$5.00	9.72%	2.90%	1.01%	1.15%	0.00%	0.12%	0.03%	0.03%	0.02%	0.00%
Log Use/Sort "I"	(spare)	$0.00	0.00%	0.00%	0.00%	0.00%	0.00%	0.00%	0.00%	0.00%	0.00%	0.00%
Log Use/Sort "J"	(spare)	$0.00	0.00%	0.00%	0.00%	0.00%	0.00%	0.00%	0.00%	0.00%	0.00%	0.00%
Log Use/Sort "K"	(spare)	$0.00	0.00%	0.00%	0.00%	0.00%	0.00%	0.00%	0.00%	0.00%	0.00%	0.00%
Log Use/Sort "L"	(spare)	$0.00	0.00%	0.00%	0.00%	0.00%	0.00%	0.00%	0.00%	0.00%	0.00%	0.00%
Log Use/Sort "M"	(spare)	$0.00	0.00%	0.00%	0.00%	0.00%	0.00%	0.00%	0.00%	0.00%	0.00%	0.00%
Log Use/Sort "N"	(spare)	$0.00	0.00%	0.00%	0.00%	0.00%	0.00%	0.00%	0.00%	0.00%	0.00%	0.00%
Log Use/Sort "O"	(spare)	$0.00	0.00%	0.00%	0.00%	0.00%	0.00%	0.00%	0.00%	0.00%	0.00%	0.00%
Log Use/Sort "P"	(spare)	$0.00	0.00%	0.00%	0.00%	0.00%	0.00%	0.00%	0.00%	0.00%	0.00%	0.00%
Log Use/Sort "Q"	(spare)	$0.00	0.00%	0.00%	0.00%	0.00%	0.00%	0.00%	0.00%	0.00%	0.00%	0.00%
Log Use/Sort "R"	(spare)	$0.00	0.00%	0.00%	0.00%	0.00%	0.00%	0.00%	0.00%	0.00%	0.00%	0.00%
Log Use/Sort "S"	(spare)	$0.00	0.00%	0.00%	0.00%	0.00%	0.00%	0.00%	0.00%	0.00%	0.00%	0.00%
Log Use/Sort "T"	(spare)	$0.00	0.00%	0.00%	0.00%	0.00%	0.00%	0.00%	0.00%	0.00%	0.00%	0.00%
Log Use/Sort "U"	(spare)	$0.00	0.00%	0.00%	0.00%	0.00%	0.00%	0.00%	0.00%	0.00%	0.00%	0.00%
Log Use/Sort "V"	(spare)	$0.00	0.00%	0.00%	0.00%	0.00%	0.00%	0.00%	0.00%	0.00%	0.00%	0.00%
Log Use/Sort "W"	(spare)	$0.00	0.00%	0.00%	0.00%	0.00%	0.00%	0.00%	0.00%	0.00%	0.00%	0.00%
Log Use/Sort "X"	(spare)	$0.00	0.00%	0.00%	0.00%	0.00%	0.00%	0.00%	0.00%	0.00%	0.00%	0.00%
Log Use/Sort "Y"	(spare)	$0.00	0.00%	0.00%	0.00%	0.00%	0.00%	0.00%	0.00%	0.00%	0.00%	0.00%
Log Use/Sort "Z"	(spare)	$0.00	0.00%	0.00%	0.00%	0.00%	0.00%	0.00%	0.00%	0.00%	0.00%	0.00%
	TOTAL >>		100.00%	100.00%	100.00%	100.00%	100.00%	100.00%	100.00%	100.00%	100.00%	100.00%

SUMMARY OF RESULTS MIXED SOFTWOOD LOGS - EXAMPLE RUN

	Ponderosa P	Douglas-fir	Pulpwood	Woods Run	(spare)
1 LOG SPECIES / GRADE					
2 DELIVERED LOG COST ($/u	$300.00	$320.00	$75.00	$180.00	$0.00
3 LOG SORTING COST ($/un	$60.00	$65.00	$95.00	$75.00	$0.00
4 LOG SCALE (unit) INPUT	720	2,760	1,980	5,240	0
5 LOG SCALE (unit) OUTPU	720	2,760	1,980	5,240	0
6 LOSS IN LOG SCALE	0.00%	0.00%	0.00%	0.00%	0.00%
7 DELIVERED LOG COST (te	$216.00	$883.20	$148.50	$943.20	$0.00
8 LOG SORTING COST (tes	$43.20	$179.40	$188.10	$393.00	$0.00
9 LOG VALUE (test)	$292.85	$1,333.60	$328.90	$1,499.30	$0.00
10 AVERAGE LOG VALUE ($/u	$406.74	$483.19	$166.11	$286.13	$0.00
11 GROSS MARGIN (test)	$33.65	$271.00	($7.70)	$163.10	$0.00
12 GROSS MARGIN ($/unit) LO	$46.74	$98.19	($3.89)	$31.13	$0.00
13 GROSS MARGIN ($/unit) LOG	$46.74	$98.19	($3.89)	$31.13	$0.00

Description of Summary Item

1. Log grade of study logs delivered to the sort yard for processing (e.g., species and/or use class).
2. Cost of logs in dollars per unit (e.g., $/unit) delivered to the sort yard.
3. Log processing cost (unload, grade, scale, sort, storage, reload) in dollars per unit (e.g., $/unit).
4. Total log scale (MBF, Cunits, Cords, Lbs., Cubic Meters) of study logs delivered.
5. Total log scale (MBF, Cunits, Cords, Lbs., Cubic Meters) of study logs after sorting.
6. Percent loss in study log scale due to handling, breakage, etc. (typically about 5%).
7. Cost of study logs delivered to yard (i.e., stumpage, harvest, and haul costs).
8. Cost of processing (unload, grade, scale, sort, storage, reload) study logs.
9. Total value of processed study logs, FOB log yard.
10. Log value in dollars per unit (e.g., $/unit).
11. Study log value minus study log costs (delivered cost + sorting cost).
12. Log value minus log cost in dollars per unit of log scale delivered.
13. Log value minus log cost in dollars per unit of log scale after sorting.

Note: Difference between #12 and #13 are attributed to losses due to handling and breakage.

GROSS MARGIN INTERPRETATION

Positive Gross Margins indicate scenarios worth further investigation and more intensive financial analysis. Negative ($.....) Gross Margins indicate nonviable scenarios and not worth further investigation. This will save considerable effort, time, and money spent chasing poor investment scenarios and help focus on the more promising opportunities.

Appendix B—Technical Assistance and Information

Technical Assistance

The Technology Marketing Unit of the Forest Products Laboratory can assist in general recommendations for log sort yards. Assistance is generally limited to technical inquiries and requests for technical publications. Onsite visits are considered on a case-by-case basis. Site visits are generally limited to providing knowledge about log sort yard and primary processing for improving utilization and processing efficiency. Log sort yard layout, design, construction, operation, and other in-depth topics are referred to consulting forestry and engineering firms.

For technical assistance and information, contact the Technology Marketing Unit, Forest Products Laboratory, USDA Forest Service, One Gifford Pinchot Drive, Madison, Wisconsin 53726. Additional information can be found on the Technology Marketing Unit website at www.fpl.fs fed.us/tmu/ and the Forest Products Laboratory website at www fpl.fs fed.us/.

For additional sources of information, refer to Appendix C.

Product Options

A good source of general information on material properties and products is the *Wood Handbook—Wood as an Engineering Material* (Forest Products Laboratory 1999). Specific information on properties and uses by tree species can be found in *Hardwoods of North America* (Alden 1995) and *Softwoods of North America* (Alden 1997).

Forest Inventory Analysis

The USDA Forest Service maintains online (Internet) forest inventory databases on timber resources, roundwood removals, and forest product production for the United States. This information is available from the Forest Inventory and Analysis (FIA) and the Timber Product Output (TPO) database retrieval systems at www.fia fs.fed.us/.

The FIA database retrieval system produces tables and maps and can be customized by geographic (timberland) (area), number of trees per acre, growing-stock volume, and other categories. The TPO database retrieval system provides county-level data on roundwood products harvested, logging residues, and wood and mill residues generated by primary wood-using mills.

Feasibility and Marketing Plans

General information on market feasibility and marketing plans is readily available from your public library and bookstores. Three recommended marketing publications specific to forest products are *A Planning Guide for Small and Medium Size Wood Products Companies: the Keys to Success* (Howe 1995), *Marketing Forest Products* (Mater 1992), and *Forest Products Marketing* (Sinclair 1992).

Small Business Assistance

Financial and business technical assistance for expansion or creation of businesses is readily available from the Small Business Administration (SBA) and Small Business Development Centers (SBDCs). Both provide a number of resources on business management issues.

The SBA provides financial, technical, and management assistance on starting, operating, and expanding businesses. With a portfolio of business loans, loan guarantees, and disaster loans worth more than $45 billion, in addition to a venture capital portfolio of $13 billion, SBA is the largest single financial backer of small businesses in the nation. For more information, contact SBA at www.sba.gov/.

Regional SBDCs can provide one-on-one assistance with business planning. SBDCs also provide business planning, marketing, and workshops for small business owners. The SBDC National Information Clearinghouse website site provides several small business resources (http://sbdcnet.utsa.edu).

Appendix C—Selected Planning Resources

Business Planning

Bangs, D.H. Jr. 1995. The business planning guide: creating a plan for success in your own business. Chicago, IL: Upstart Publishing Company, Inc., a Division of Dearborn Publishing Group, Inc. 208 p.

Entrepreneur Magazine. 1995. Small business advisor. New York, NY: John Wiley & Sons, Inc. 664 p.

Howe, J.; Bratkovich, S. 1995. A planning guide for small and medium size wood products companies: the keys to success. NA–TP–09–95. U.S. St. Paul, MN: Department of Agriculture, Forest Service, Northeastern Area, State & Private Forestry.

Forest Products Marketing

Cesa, E.T. 1992. A marketing guide for manufacturers and entrepreneurs of secondary-processed wood products in the northeastern United States. NA–TP–09–92. U.S. St. Paul, MN: Department of Agriculture, Forest Service, Northeastern Area, State & Private Forestry. Northeastern Area. 85 p.

Leckey, D. 1998. Buying and selling softwood lumber; a guide to the lumber market of North America. Eugene, OR. Random Lengths Publications, Inc. 228 p.

Mater, J.; Mater, M.S.; Mater, C .M. 1992. Marketing forest products. San Francisco, CA: Miller Freeman, Inc. 290 p.

Sinclair, S.A. 1992. Forest products marketing. New York, NY: McGraw–Hill, Inc. 403 p.

Forest Products Market Reports

Random Lengths. Weekly report on North American softwood forest products markets.

    Random Lengths Publications, Inc.
    P.O. Box 867, Eugene, Oregon 97440–0867
    Phone: 541–686–9925; Fax: 800–686–9925
    E-mail: rlmail@randomlengths.com
    Website: www randomlengths.com

Hardwood Market Report. Weekly report on North American hardwood lumber markets.

    Hardwood Market Report
    P.O. Box 241325, Memphis, TN 38124–1325
    Phone: 901–767–9126; Fax: 901–767–7534
    E-mail: hmr@hmr.com
    Website: www hmr.com

Forest Industry Trade Magazines

Canadian Forest Industries
JCFT Forest Communications
90 Morgan, Unit 14
Baie d'Urfe', Quebec, Canada H9X 3A8
Phone: 514–457–2211; Fax: 574–457–2558

Forest Products Equipment
P.O. Box 621
Twin City, GA 30471
Phone: 912–763–3500
Website: www.forestproductsequip.com

The Logger and Lumberman Magazine
P.O. Box 489
Wadley, GA 30477
Phone: 478–252–5237; Fax: 478–252–1140
Website: www.loggerandlumberman.com

Logging and Sawmilling Journal (Canadian)
P.O. Box 86670
North Vancouver, BC V7L 1B4
Phone: 604–990–9970; Fax: 604–990–9971
Website: www.forestnet.com

Southern Lumberman
P.O. Box 681629
Franklin, TN 37068–1629
Phone: 615–791–1961; Fax: 615–591–1035
Website: www.southernlumberman.com

Timber Processing
P.O. Box 5613
Montgomery, AL 36103–5613
Phone: 334–834–1170; Fax: 334–834–4825
Website: www.timberprocessing.com

Industry Directory

Random Lengths Publications. 2003. Big book: the buyers and sellers directory of the forest products industry. Eugene, OR: Random Lengths Publications, Inc. 1,024 p.

Log-Sort Yards (General)

Dramm, J.R.; Jackson, G.; Wong, J. 2002. Review of log sort yards. FPL–GTR–132. Madison, WI: U.S. Department of Agriculture, Forest Service, Forest Products Laboratory. 39 p.

Hampton, C.M. 1981. Dry land log handling and sorting: planning, constructing, and operation of log yards. San Francisco, CA: Miller Freeman Publications, Inc. 215 p.

Sinclair, A.W.J.; Wellburn, G.V. 1984. A handbook for designing, building, and operating a log sort yard. Vancouver, BC. Canada: Forest Engineering Research Institute of Canada. 285 p

Related References

Baldwin, R.F. 1984. Operations management in the forest products industry. San Francisco, CA: Miller Freeman Publications. 264 p.

Hoffman, B.F. 1991. How to improve logging profits. Old Forge, NY: Northeastern Loggers Association, Inc. 64 p.

Tooch, D.E. 1992. Managing for profit: successful sawmill management. Old Forge, NY: Northeastern Loggers Association, Inc. 204 p.